D0795585

Rose Reisman Brings Home Pasta Dishes

Rose Reisman Brings Home Pasta Dishes

Healthful Pasta Recipes from Top Restaurants Made Easy

by Rose Reisman

Andrews and McMeel

A Universal Press Syndicate Company

Kansas City

Library of Congress Cataloging-in-Publication Data

Reisman, Rose.
    Rose Reisman brings home pasta dishes / Rose Reisman.
      p. cm.
    Includes index.
    ISBN 0–8362–2106–0 (pbk.) : $12.95
    1. Cookery (Pasta) I. Title.
TX809.M17R46   1991
641.8'22—dc20   91–27953
                                                CIP

Book design by Rick Cusick

Attention: Schools and Businesses
Andrews and McMeel books are available at quantity discounts with bulk purchase for educational, business, or sales promotional use. For information, please write to: Special Sales Department, Andrews and McMeel, 4900 Main Street, Kansas City, Missouri 64112.

My fourth cookbook, as my other three, is dedicated to my family—my husband, Sam, and three children, Natalie, David, and Laura.

I would like to thank my husband and congratulate him for his indefatigable appetite for having had to endure six pastas per day for eight weeks on end. Not many were up to the challenge; I knew that he was. If not for his constant praise, criticism, and support throughout all of my work, I seriously doubt my career would have progressed even this far. Balancing my career and home life would not have been the challenge it is without my children, from whom and on whom I have derived and expended my drive and energy.

And finally, to the woman who may not have taught me everything I know about cooking but who has always been a supporter of all my endeavors, my mother, Mary.

Contents

Acknowledgments

Photography by Mark Shapiro (In-Camera Studio)
Photo design director, Don Fernley.
Food stylist, Kate Bush.
Props by Rose Reisman.
Tableware donated by Villeroy and Boch Ltd. in Toronto.
Tableware donated by Grant's Fine China and Gifts in Toronto.
Tableware donated by Junors in Toronto.
Materials donated by B. B. Bargoon's in Toronto.
Glassblock and tile donated by Thames Valley Brick and Tile Inc.
Editing by Dolly Jenkinson.
A thanks to Vivian Birchall and Barbara Spiess for assistance in the testing
    kitchen.

This is my fourth cookbook in as many years, and my first outside of a dessert-based one. To take on pasta is a new and important challenge for me—important because my ambition is to establish myself as a serious writer of cookbooks and to do this successfully means expanding my repertoire. Pasta represents the second step in fulfilling this goal.

My goal is to collect and simplify otherwise excellent but difficult expert recipes, and I am now satisfied that this book has accomplished that mission. Initially, I was intimidated because of the newness of the subject. Now, however, I have concluded that desserts, not pastas, have proven to be the more difficult area of food preparation—ingredients must be measured more precisely, baking times must be exact, and the techniques employed generally require a greater level of knowledge and expertise. The result is great news for the users of this book, as everyone, whether or not initiated in the art of cooking, will find that the results of their efforts compare favorably with those of the experts.

Why pasta? There was no magic in the selection; I wanted to choose an important staple in the North American diet. Subsequent books will, undoubtedly, cover areas like chicken, seafood, and fish, among others, but it appears to me that North America is having a love affair with pasta so the time is opportune.

In the North American context, pasta was popularized and used almost exclusively by Italian immigrants and was considered a cheap bulk food, prepared with butter and cheese or a dollop of tomato sauce. Since the 1970s, pasta consumption has been steadily on the increase. According to recent statistics published by the U.S. Department of Commerce and Bureau of the Census, the annual per capita consumption of pasta products rose from 11.3 pounds in 1975 to 18.4 pounds in 1990. Prepackaged pasta production rose from 1.4 million pounds in 1970 to 3.8 million pounds in 1989. It is available in a myriad of shapes and colors and can be stored for several months in its dried form. Fresh pasta, once frozen, is best used within a three-month period.

Over time, as diet came under increasing scrutiny by the health- and fitness-minded alike, our understanding of good eating habits matured, and pasta was identified as an inexpensive food, high in carbohydrates and low in fat. This excellent and versatile source of nourishment has become a staple for the North American population, displacing the historically high beef content in our diets. Carefully prepared, pasta not only provides an excellent source of carbohydrates, but, combined with meat, seafood, fish or chicken, vegetables, and cheese, it becomes a total, nutritious meal.

Pasta can be anything you want it to be. It's an amazingly simple food consisting mainly of flour, water, and eggs. Other ingredients, such as tomatoes, spinach, and herbs, may be added to the dough for extra flavor and color. It may be prepared with tomato sauce as a simple side dish, or added to for a more substantial meal. And the ever-popular macaroni and cheese is always an acceptable meal to children of all ages.

Only restaurants of discriminating quality from across North America have been selected for inclusion in this book. There are over 150 pasta recipes from 48 top-rated restaurants whose chefs have carefully chosen some of their most prized dishes. A special selection of nutritionally ana-lyzed, low-fat, low-cholesterol recipes have also been included, and all recipes have been tested at least three times in my kitchen and adapted for the home kitchen. Most can be prepared in less than 30 minutes, and ingredients and utensils are easily available. And for those who travel exten-sively, a concise descriptive background of each establishment has been provided.

Bring home the pasta, and enjoy the experience!

Cooking Pasta

Begin with a pot that can easily hold about 3 quarts of water for each 8-oz. package of dried pasta. Add ½–1 tbsp. salt and 1 tbsp. of oil to prevent the pasta from sticking. Heat the water until boiling and then add the pasta slowly. Only stir if the pasta needs to be separated, otherwise leave it to cook. Boil, uncovered, until "al dente," firm to the bite, or still chewy. Times vary according to the type of pasta; beware of the timing instructions on the package.

Once the pasta is cooked, drain it quickly in a colander and run cold water through it if it is to be used in a cold pasta salad, or to facilitate handling. A little water in the pasta will combine easily with the added sauce, so don't worry about straining the water thoroughly. If the pasta is to be used later in a hot dish, toss it with a little oil or butter or some of the sauce called for in the recipe to prevent it from sticking.

How Much to Cook

Two oz. of dried pasta makes approximately 1 cup of cooked pasta.
One-half lb. of dry pasta will serve between 2 and 4 people, depending upon whether it is being served as an appetizer or main meal.
One lb. of dry pasta usually serves between 4 and 6 people, again depending upon whether it is an appetizer or main course.

Types of Pastas

There are so many varieties of fresh and dry pastas that it is easy to be confused about which type to pair with a particular sauce. Some master pasta chefs have strict guidelines, but pasta is flexible, so break the rules and combine whatever pasta you like with a sauce that suits you. Generally speaking, relatively thick pastas are better with robust sauces and baked pastas. Thin strand pastas are best with lighter sauces. Unusual shaped pastas suit lighter sauces so their shapes are not lost. Remember to buy good pasta to start with, either from an excellent manufacturer of dried pasta, or a specialty store that makes its own on site. Good dry pasta is always better than stale "fresh" pasta.

Below is a list of some of the common dry pastas called for in the following recipes. All of them can be found in grocery stores.

3

Agnolotti

This pasta looks like ravioli and is usually semicircular or square. It is filled with various ingredients such as cheese, meat, or vegetables. You can substitute any stuffed pasta, such as ravioli or tortellini.

Bucatini

This is a thin spaghetti with a hole through the middle. Use it as you would spaghetti.

Cannelloni

These are approximately 4″ × 5″ pieces of fresh pasta or dry, rolled pasta. They can be filled with meat or cheese fillings and are usually baked in a sauce. They are smaller than manicotti shells, but can be used interchangeably with them. Approximately 1 tbsp. of filling is appropriate for each shell.

Capellini (fedilini, spaghettini)

"Fine hairs" pasta, which is usually sold coiled. Angel hair pasta is even thinner.

Conchiglie (shells)

These are small to large pasta shells that can be stuffed with meat, cheese, or vegetable fillings. If a recipe calls for stuffed pastas such as ravioli or tortellini and there is not the time to prepare, the large conchiglie (shells) are an ideal substitute.

Farfalle (bow ties)

These resemble butterflies. They come in different sizes, but are usually used in the same way as a wide, flat noodle.

Fettuccine (tagliatelle)

Flat pasta $1/4$″ to $3/8$″ wide.

4

Fusilli (spiral pasta)

These are approximately 3″ long pieces of pasta that look like twisted spaghetti or corkscrews.

Gnocchi

This pasta looks like dumplings. Make your own and freeze them, or buy the packaged gnocchi, which are usually excellent. Gnocchi is made from potatoes and flour, and can be served with a variety of sauces.

Lasagna

Long and wide dry pasta usually 13″ × 3″ used in baked dishes. Fresh sheets of pasta can be used, cut to the desired length.

Linguine

This pasta is thinner than fettuccine and wider than spaghetti.

Macaroni (elbow)

These are short, curved tubes of pasta used for casseroles or soups.

Manicotti

These are larger tubes of pasta than cannelloni, and are usually filled with a cheese mixture and baked with a sauce. You can buy them dry and rolled, or buy sheets of lasagna and cut to desired size, usually 5″ × 4″. If a recipe calls for stuffed pasta, such as tortellini or ravioli, these pasta rolls can be substituted. Approximately 1 tbsp. of filling in each shell.

Orzo

This form of pasta is sometimes used as a substitute for rice. It resembles rice but is heavier and fuller. It is good in soups.

Penne (rigate)

Diagonally cut pieces of tubular pasta 2″ long. Good with heavier meat sauces.

Ravioli

These are square pieces of pasta approximately 1″ to 2″ wide, filled with a small amount of cheese or meat filling. You can prepare your own or buy ready-made frozen. Serve with a sauce. The fillings for this pasta can be substituted in manicotti, cannelloni, or jumbo pasta shells.

Rigatoni

These are 1½″ long tubes of pasta with ridges. These are excellent with a chunky sauce.

Risotto

This is an Italian rice. If not available, regular good-quality rice can be substituted.

Spaghetti

This is the most well-known pasta, coming in many sizes from thin capellini to thick spaghettoni.

Tagliatelle

This is similar to fettuccine.

Tortellini

This resembles ravioli, but instead of square, this stuffed pasta is twisted and filled with cheese or meat. You can prepare your own or use ready-made frozen. The fillings for this pasta can be substituted in manicotti, cannelloni, or jumbo pasta shells.

Ziti

This is tubular macaroni similar to penne.

Making Fresh Pasta by Hand or Machine

I have found that since pasta is such a popular food item, the varieties of dry pasta are excellent. And the fresh pasta sections of groceries have grown significantly to carry many different types of shapes, flavors, and colors of pasta. But many people still enjoy making their own pasta. Keep in mind that it takes time and patience, but is well worth the effort.

Basic Pasta Dough
(3–4 servings—makes approximately ³⁄₄ lb.)

2 large eggs
³⁄₄ tbsp. oil
1¹⁄₂ cups flour
pinch salt

Beat eggs and oil in a bowl. Sift the flour and salt over the eggs. Mix with a fork and form into a ball. If it is too sticky, add some flour until it is easy to handle. If too dry, add some water. Knead for approximately 8 minutes, until smooth. Wrap in a slightly moistened towel and let rest approximately 30 minutes on the counter before rolling and cutting into various pasta shapes.

You can also use a food processor or electric mixer by adding the flour to the bowl, turning on the motor, and at the same time adding the eggs and oil and running until the dough becomes a ball. If too sticky, add more flour; if too dry, add a few drops of water. Knead for approximately 5 minutes until smooth. Let rest for 30 minutes.

A more classic way of making pasta is to mound the flour on a table. Make a well and break the eggs into it. Add oil and with a fork begin to slowly gather the flour from the sides into the middle until all is incorporated. Follow the same directions as above.

Some flavorful and colorful variations to the pasta can be added quite simply. Just add the following ingredients and continue with the same method of making the basic pasta dough.

Tomato Pasta

Add 2 tbsp. tomato paste to basic pasta dough. Add more flour if too sticky.

Green Pasta (Pasta Verdi)

Chop finely 8 oz. of well-drained, fresh, cooked spinach. Use only 1 egg in basic pasta dough. If too wet, add extra flour.

Herb Pasta

Chop 2 tbsp. of any herb of your choice and add to basic pasta dough.

Whole Wheat Pasta

Use 1 cup whole wheat flour and ¼ cup white flour in place of 1½ cups white flour in basic pasta dough, keeping in mind this produces a heavier pasta. For a lighter version, substitute half whole wheat flour and half white flour.

Black Pepper Pasta

Add 2 tsp. freshly ground black pepper to basic pasta dough.

Garlic Pasta

Finely chop 5 cloves of garlic and add to basic pasta dough along with 1 tbsp. of water.

Semolina Pasta

Probably this is the best tasting dough to make pasta. Substitute semolina flour for all-purpose flour in basic pasta dough. This is very hard to knead and can tend to clog the holes of electric machines. So use with care.

Black Pasta

Use only 1 egg in basic pasta dough. Mix 2 tbsp. squid ink with ¼ cup water. Combine squid ink mixture with the other ingredients and process in the usual manner.

Rolling the Dough by Hand or Machine

Hand rolling with a pin can be tricky. Success may come best from pasta machines, either manual or electric.

Rolling Pasta by Hand

A long rolling pin and fairly large working space is essential. Work quickly or the pasta will crack and dry. Roll the dough away from you, stretching it as you roll. After each roll, give the dough a quarter turn to keep the circular shape. If the dough is sticking to the counter, add a little flour to the surface. Pull and stretch the dough instead of rolling it. To stretch it, place the dough on top of the rolling pin and pull carefully. When the dough gets very large, let it hang over the counter to stretch more. In a few minutes the dough will look smooth and should be very thin, approximately 1⁄8" thick. If the dough is to be used for unfilled pasta, spread it on a towel to dry for approximately 30 minutes. Use it immediately for filled pasta such as ravioli or tortellini.

Now the dough is ready to cut into shapes of your choice. You can either do this with a knife and by hand, or you can use a manual or electric pasta machine.

Pasta Machines

Two types of wringer-style pasta machines are available: One has a motor and the other is turned by hand.

Manual Machine

After the dough is rested, divide into 3 or 4 pieces. Keep the pieces not being used wrapped in plastic. Flatten a piece of dough with your hand just so that it will fit through the pasta machine at the widest setting. Feed the pasta into the machine with one hand while working the machine with the other hand. After it comes out, fold it over and refeed the machine. When the dough begins to get smooth and elastic, start to narrow the roller openings. Continue this process until the dough achieves the desired thickness. Lay the pieces on a well-floured surface. If the dough stays out too long, cover it with a towel. Now attach the cutting attachment desired to the pasta machine. Follow the manufacturer's instructions. Sprinkle the freshly cut pasta in some flour, toss in a pile, or gather in strands. Now you can lay the pasta on a drying rack, place it in the refrigerator or freezer in a plastic bag, or cook it immediately in boiling water. In the refrigerator it will stay fresh for approximately 1 week, in the freezer for 1 to 2 months.

Extrusion Machines (electric)

An electric machine pushes the dough through a die that comes out with a shape. In the more elaborate machines, you place your ingredients in an opening at the top of the machine and the machine kneads it. After a few minutes it comes out the other end in various shapes, depending upon the attachment affixed. Common problems with these machines is that the flour tends to clog in the holes of the various attachments, and the time cleaning the holes can be considerable.

Various Shapes to Cut by Hand

Fettuccine (tagliatelle) or any flat noodle

Roll up the dough like a jellyroll and cut in even widths to desired shape, approximately ¼" thick. Cook immediately or let dry for a few days before storing.

Manicotti, Cannelloni, Lasagna

Cut flat sheets of pasta to width and length desired. (5" × 4" is the most common for manicotti or cannelloni). Cook for only about 2 to 3 minutes in boiling water with some oil. Do not place too many in pot, or they may stick together. Drain and rinse with cold water to prevent sticking. These sheets can be filled with meat, cheese, or vegetable stuffings, and later covered and baked with a sauce over top so the pasta does not dry out. If you want to store the sheets before using, package them by laying plastic or wax paper in between the layers. Freeze for as long as 2 months, refrigerate for about 1 week, or best of all, cook immediately.

Stuffed or Filled Pasta—Ravioli (round, square), Tortellini

Prepare the desired filling and set aside. Roll the pasta dough into strips approximately 12" long × 4" wide. Keep the unused strips covered with a damp towel. Brush the strip of dough with a little beaten egg. Place a small amount of filling (approximately ½ tsp.) at approximately 1½" intervals over the pasta, depending upon the size of the filled pasta required. Lay a second sheet over top and press down firmly. For square shapes, cut between the fillings with a knife, pastry wheel, or special pasta cutter.

For round shapes, cut circles of a desired width (approximately 1"–2"). For tortellini, cut 2" circles, place a small amount of filling off to one side of the circle. Fold over one side so it falls a little short of the other side. Bend together and push the edges together.

There are also marked rolling pins for making filled pasta or ravioli trays. Use whatever you are used to.

Fine Strands Pasta (spaghetti, vermicelli, angel hair, etc.)

These pastas are best bought dried because cutting them so thin is very difficult.

Important Ingredients

Butter or Margarine

Unsalted butter has a fresher and healthier taste. It can be kept frozen so that you can always have it on hand. If cholesterol is a concern, substitute a good-quality vegetable margarine.

Cheeses

There is never the perfect cheese for a specific pasta meal. The recipes give recommendations, but feel free to substitute. If you feel a cheese is too strong, substitute a milder cheese and vice versa. Below is a list of common cheeses used with pasta. If fat or cholesterol is a concern, there are now available low-fat cheeses with only 15% butterfat instead of 30% butterfat.

The Best Hard Cheeses for Grating

Parmesan

Parmesan cheese is probably the most common cheese used with pasta. It is always better to buy it fresh and grate it yourself. If you need grated cheese on hand, most groceries have a deli department where they sell it freshly grated. The prepackaged grated cheese is not as fresh and does not use the best parmigiana cheeses. Parmesan should have a good golden color, which indicates a well-aged cheese, not a pale color, which indicates a younger cheese. The best Parmesan will be labeled "Parmigiano-Reggiano."

Asiago

A hard, dry cheese with a strong flavor.

Romano

Very sharp and salty. If you do not like the taste, substitute Parmesan.

Aged Provolone

A pear-shaped cheese. The aging gives it a strong taste.

Aged Gouda

Hard and tasty.

Soft Fresh Cheeses

Ricotta

Creamy and bland. Use in place of cottage cheese, cream cheese, or mascarpone cheese.

Cottage

White, soft curds. Ricotta or cream cheese can be substituted.

Cream Cheese

Soft and creamy. Ricotta, cottage, or mascarpone cheese can be substituted.

Mascarpone Cheese

A delicious double cream, soft and creamy Italian cheese usually used in Tiramisu, an Italian dessert. Can be substituted with cream cheese or ricotta.

Goat Cheese (chevre)

Distinctive flavor, made from goat's milk.

Blue Cheeses

Includes Roquefort, Gorgonzola, Danish Blue, and Stilton. Soft and creamy with a blue mold. Very distinct flavor. It is usually used in combination with a milder cheese.

Semi-Soft Cheeses and Bland Cheeses

Mozzarella

Creamy, mild, and sweet.

Gruyère

Type of Swiss cheese. Delicate flavor and tasty. Sweeter than Emmentaler.

Emmentaler

Type of Swiss cheese. Firm texture with a pleasant, nutty flavor.

Jarlsberg

Type of Swiss cheese. Nutty, Swiss-like flavor. An excellent cooking and eating cheese.

Fontina

Creamy and buttery whole fat cheese. Any mild cheese can be substituted.

Muenster

Creamy and bland. Any creamy, mild cheese can be substituted.

Monterey Jack

Soft and mild. Any mild cheese can be substituted.

Havarti

Mild and sweet. Any mild cheese can be substituted.

Brie

Soft, mild, and sweet cheese.

Garlic

Fresh, whole garlic is always the best to use. Store it in a dry, airy spot. Powder garlic or garlic salt should not be used if a true garlic taste is required. Chopped garlic in a jar of oil can be quite good, but the fullest garlic flavor comes from only freshly squeezed garlic cloves.

Oil

First pressed, extra virgin olive oil is the best oil to use because of its rich, fruity consistency. The first pressing is important because there has been no addition of heat or chemicals to the oil. The darker the oil, the richer the olive taste. If this flavor is too strong for you, select a lighter oil for a more subtle taste.

Herbs

Fresh herbs such as basil, oregano, and parsley are most commonly used for pasta dishes. Fresh is always preferred to dry, but when not in season, dried herbs, as long as they have been kept in airtight jars and stored in a dry cool place, will suffice. The recipes include measurements for both fresh and dry herbs.

Tomatoes, Tomato Pasta, and Tomato Concentrate

Many of the recipes call for chopped tomatoes. When in season, fresh tomatoes are best. Chop them and try to save the juice for the sauce. When tomatoes are not in season, it is better to use canned tomatoes, preferably Italian plum. Weigh them without the extra juice, just as you would fresh tomatoes, and place them right in the pan. They will break up during the cooking process if you stir occasionally. Do not chop them beforehand or you will lose the juices. Add the juice from the can only if the recipe calls for it.

Try not to use canned tomato sauce or seasoned tomatoes because the seasoning is not fresh.

Tomato paste, a concentrate form of tomatoes, adds great flavor to sauces, as well as thickening the sauce.

Tomato concentrate comes in a tube and is twice as intense as the paste. It has a better flavor than the paste and leaves no bitter taste afterward.

Fresh and Dried Mushrooms

Many of the recipes call for small amounts of specific dried mushrooms, such as porcini, shiitake, or chanterelles. These delicacies can be found in the gourmet section of a supermarket or in Italian groceries. They usually come in sizes of 1–2 oz. bags or jars and can range in price anywhere from $3.00 to $20.00, depending upon the type. Most recipes call for only 1 oz. The mushrooms must be soaked in approximately 1 cup of warm water or stock for 30 minutes. Drain well and use as is.

If you do not want to use these high-priced items, feel free to use fresh mushrooms in their place. Usually, 1 oz. dry mushrooms equals 8 oz. fresh. If using fresh, try to obtain wild mushrooms such as oyster, chanterelle, or shiitake, instead of the common kind.

Artichokes

Many of the recipes call for this vegetable. You can use canned or cook your own. Cook them in boiling, salted water or a dry white wine that has been flavored with herbs and oil, just until tender, approximately 30 minutes for larger hearts. Test doneness by pulling off an outer leaf. If it pulls off easily, the artichoke is ready. Peel off leaves until you reach the heart.

Basic Sauces and Stocks

The following sauces, as well as those in the book, can be refrigerated or frozen if they are not to be used immediately. In the refrigerator they can be kept for at least 1 week, and in the freezer for up to 3 months.

White Sauce or Bechamel

3 tbsp. butter
4 tbsp. flour
2 cups chicken stock
pepper and salt to taste
dash of nutmeg
1 cup heavy cream

Melt butter in small pot. Add flour and cook approx. 2 minutes, until smooth. Add stock and stir continuously until thick. Simmer for 2 minutes.

Add seasoning and cream and simmer for 2 more minutes. Spoon over pasta in quantity desired. Remainder can be reserved for later use.

Alfredo (Use 1 lb. fettuccine or any flat pasta) Serves 4–6

⅔ cup unsalted butter (soft)
1⅓ cups heavy cream
1½ cups grated Parmesan cheese

Heat the butter and cream over a medium-low heat, just until the butter is all melted and the mixture becomes hot. Slowly add 1 cup of the cheese until it has melted and the sauce has thickened. Divide among plates and add the extra cheese over top. Season with fresh black pepper.

Basic Tomato Sauce (Use 1 lb. tagliatelle or spaghetti) Serves 4–6

There are many variations of tomato sauce, including cooked and uncooked, and ones with the addition of several spices. This is just a basic sauce. Use it as a basis for your sauce and add to it.

2 tbsp. olive oil
1 onion, chopped
3 cloves crushed garlic
1 (28-oz.) can plum tomatoes
¾ cup Parmesan cheese

Heat the oil and add the onion and garlic and cook until soft. Add the tomatoes in their juice and cook, uncovered, on a high heat, stirring occasionally, for approx. 15–20 minutes. The sauce should now be thickened. Process until smooth. Add to cooked pasta and add Parmesan cheese. Season with fresh pepper.

Basil Pesto (Use over 1 lb. fine to medium strands of pasta such as angel hair, linguine, spaghetti, fettuccine, etc.) Serves 4–6

This is a classic pesto sauce that can be varied by substituting your favorite nuts for pine nuts, and other greens, such as parsley or spinach, for the basil leaves.

$^2\!/_3$ cup toasted pine nuts
3 cups fresh basil leaves, well-packed
1$^1\!/_3$ cups olive oil
3 large garlic cloves
1$^1\!/_4$ cups Parmesan cheese

Place all of the above ingredients into a food processor and grind until smooth. Serve with hot pasta.

Sun-Dried Tomato Pesto (Serve over 1 lb. fine to medium pasta) Serves 4–6

Sun-dried tomatoes can be bought at gourmet food stores, packed in olive oil or packaged dry. You can marinate them yourself in jars of olive oil. Keep them in a cool, dry place. They keep forever!

3 cups sun-dried tomatoes, drained and well-packed
1$^1\!/_4$ cups olive oil
$^1\!/_4$ cup oil from the sun-dried tomatoes
1 cup grated Parmesan cheese
$^3\!/_4$ cup toasted pine nuts
$^3\!/_4$ cup well-packed parsley leaves
4 cloves of garlic

Place all of the above into a food processor. Grind until the sauce is fairly smooth. Toss with cooked pasta.

Stocks (chicken, beef or fish)

Make your own stock. It's simple and yields the best results:

In 3 quarts of water, boil a variety of vegetables such as carrots, onions, celery, and add your favorite spices. Add 2 lbs. of chicken, beef, or fish bones and simmer for 2 hours. Strain and the broth is ready to use or can be frozen for up to two months.

If homemade broth is unavailable, use: canned consommés or bouillon cubes for chicken or beef broth, bottled clam juice or clam water from a can of clams for fish broth.

Pastas Low in Calories, Cholesterol, and Fat

Pasta itself is not high in fat, calories, or cholesterol. One cup of plain cooked pasta is approximately 175 calories. The extra calories come from the sauces and other ingredients added.

A cream or butter sauce can increase the calories to 450 per serving. It is best to use tomato- and vegetable-based sauces if one wants to avoid excessive fat intake.

I have included 16 recipes from some of North America's finest spas, which meet all of the criteria of healthy living. These pastas are all nutritionally analyzed with breakdowns per serving of calories, protein, fat, cholesterol, carbohydrates, sodium, and fiber. The taste is excellent without the extra fat and calories.

Nutritional Analysis of Pasta Recipes

Pasta is a healthy meal, at times representing an excellent source of protein and carbohydrates, depending upon the ingredients involved.

At times, though, the calories of each pasta meal can be acceptable, according to one's daily calorie intake, but the fat can be excessive.

This book contains an entire section on low-fat, low-calorie pastas. Therefore, when fat and cholesterol is a concern, these recipes fit the bill.

The nutritional analysis has been provided so as to permit one to monitor their intake of calories, protein, fat, cholesterol, carbohydrates, and sodium.

The remainder of pasta dishes in the book are also nutritionally analyzed, and if fat is a concern, there are methods to lower the fat, which will be mentioned in the next section.

But first, I have provided a chart that indicates acceptable amounts of fat, protein, and carbohydrates in one's daily diet. This chart seems to be the consensus among spa nutritionists.

First, determine what your caloric intake should be with respect to your sex, age, and level of daily activity. (Your doctor can advise you on your caloric intake.)

Calorie Intake	Grams Protein per day	Grams Fat per day	Grams Carbohydrate per day
1200	45	40	165
1500	56	50	206
1800	68	60	248
2100	79	70	289
2300	86	77	316
2600	98	87	357
2900	109	97	399
3200	120	107	440

Fat

Diets that are high in saturated fats can, according to some medical experts, lead to higher blood cholesterol levels, clogged arteries, and eventually to heart disease or stroke.

Saturated fats, which are those that raise the cholesterol, are found in cheese, butter, milk, lard, and meat products. Polyunsaturated fats, found in vegetable oils and margarines, can lower cholesterol.

Monounsaturated fats that are found in olive, peanut, and canola oil also can lower blood cholesterol.

The consensus among nutritionists suggests that the ideal amount of total fat intake is 30% of your total calories. Most North Americans consume approximately 40% of their calories from fat.

A healthy amount of fat for a day should be approximately 70 grams for women and 95 grams for men. [*]

Low-fat Alternatives for Pasta Recipes

1. When selecting your fish, chicken, and beef, try to buy lean meat. Your butcher can provide this service. Excess fat is unnecessary and provides wasted grams of fat.
2. Higher fat milk products such as cheese, sour cream, and cream have large amounts of fat. Either cut back, as much as half the amount asked for in the recipe, or substitute with lower-fat products.

[*]Lindsay, Anne, *Lighthearted Everyday Cooking*, (Toronto, Canada: 1991) p. 7.

Below is a list of common high- and low-fat ingredients and their calories, fat, and cholesterol counts.

Approximate amounts	Calories	Grams of fat	Cholesterol
4 oz. butter	800	90	248 mg
4 oz. margarine	800	90	0 mg
½ cup heavy cream	410	44	160 mg
½ cup light cream (coffee cream)	230	23	80 mg
½ cup half and half	175	14	45 mg
½ cup sour cream	250	24	50 mg
½ cup light sour cream	120	8	20 mg
½ cup homogenized milk	75	4	15 mg
½ cup 2% milk	60	3	7 mg
½ cup 1% milk	50	1	5 mg
1 oz. cream cheese	100	10	30 mg
1 oz. hard cheese	110	9	30 mg
½ cup cottage cheese (4%)	120	5	20 mg
½ cup cottage cheese (2%)	100	3	17 mg
½ cup cottage cheese (1%)	90	1	5 mg
1 tbsp. oil	120	13	0 mg

For each of these groupings, the higher-fat ingredients can be reduced by as much as a third without compromising the quality of the pasta. Additionally or alternatively, substitutions can be made by using the lower-fat ingredients in each category. The resulting reduction in fat or calories can be calculated in any dish.

Other Tips to Lessen Fat

1. Use a vegetable spray to grease your skillet instead of oil or butter, keeping in mind that each tablespoon of oil and butter will save you more than 100 calories and 13 grams of fat, and 90 grams of fat, respectively.
2. Many hard cheeses are now being made with a lower fat content

(approximately 15% butterfat). Normal hard cheeses have approximately 30% butterfat.

3. When small amounts of heavy cream are called for in recipes, substitute light cream or milk.

4. When larger amounts of heavy cream are called for (½ cup or more), substitute either 18% cream, or use the equivalent of a white or bechamel sauce (see page 00), using milk, not cream.

5. Limit your protein to approximately 3 oz. per serving by cutting back on the amount otherwise indicated.

$$3 \text{ oz. of poultry } = \ 5 \text{ grams of fat}$$
$$3 \text{ oz. of lean fish } = \ 2 \text{ grams of fat}$$
$$3 \text{ oz. of fatty fish } = \ 7 \text{ grams of fat}$$
$$3 \text{ oz. of lean meat } = 10 \text{ grams of fat}$$

Select recipes with lean meat or fish instead of sausage recipes, which are very high in fat.

One should be able to achieve, depending on the dish, at least a reduction of a third and as much as half of the fat and calorie amounts.

Here's an example of how substituting or reducing high-fat ingredients can greatly alter a recipe.

Ristorante Primavera
Page 148 Tortellini with Prosciutto and Peas

(as is)

1 lb. tortellini
*4 tbsp. butter
4 slices ham
*1½ cups cream
½ cup peas
½ cup Parmesan cheese

Per serving

Calories: 473
Fat: 38 g

(with low-fat alteration)

1 lb. tortellini
*2 tbsp. butter
4 slices ham
*1½ cups half and half
½ cup peas
½ cup Parmesan cheese

Per serving

Calories: 323
Fat: 22 g

*Reduce butter to 2 tbsp., reducing 200 calories in overall recipe, and fat by 24 grams.

*Substitute heavy cream with half and half, reducing the total calories by 700 calories and fat by 80 grams.

Four Cheese Macaroni

*This can be served as a simple
or sophisticated meal. Children love it.*

Serves 4–6

8 oz. mozzarella cheese **4 oz. cheddar cheese** **4 oz. Swiss cheese** **(preferably Gruyère)**	Finely dice half of each cheese and grate the other half of each cheese.
¾ cup Parmesan cheese	Add Parmesan to grated cheese. Keep diced and grated cheeses separate.
¾ lb. macaroni	Cook in boiling salted water until firm to the bite (al dente). Drain and place in a serving dish. Add the diced cheeses and *half* of the grated cheeses, and toss well.
2 tbsp. melted butter **salt and pepper to taste**	Add to above and mix quickly. Sprinkle the remaining grated cheeses on top.
2 tbsp. melted butter	Dribble butter over top. Serve immediately.

Per serving (⅙th)

Calories:	570
Protein:	29 g
Fat:	29 g
Cholesterol:	87 mg
Carbohydrates:	44 g
Sodium:	913 mg

Penne with Bell Peppers, Mushrooms, and Cheese

This dish has an array of colors with the red and yellow peppers, green lettuce, and toasted pine nuts. The light cheese sauce blends well with this combination.

Serves 6–8 as an appetizer

¹/₂ cup pine nuts	Toast on stove or in oven at 400°F until brown. Set aside.
2 small red or yellow or green peppers (or any combination)	Broil in oven for approx. 10 minutes, until charred, turning often so as not to burn the skin. Cool, then peel skin. Remove top and seeds, and cut into strips. Set aside.
approx. 2 oz. (or small bunch) arugula * (optional)	Chop finely and set aside.
1 lb. penne pasta (short tube)	Cook in boiling water until al dente (firm to the bite). Drain and set aside. Meanwhile, prepare sauce.
2 tbsp. olive oil	Heat in skillet.
¹/₂ onion, sliced 2 crushed garlic cloves 1 green onion, chopped 1 cup chopped mushrooms	Add and sauté until golden brown.
2 tbsp. white wine	Add to above and blend.

Per serving (¹/₈th)	
Calories:	619
Protein:	16 g
Fat:	40 g
Cholesterol:	92 mg
Carbohydrates:	50 g
Sodium:	369 mg

*Arugula is a soft, leafy type of lettuce. Spinach or other leafy lettuce can be substituted.

Penne with Bell Peppers, Mushrooms, and Cheese *(continued)*

²/₃ cup chicken broth	Add and cook until slightly reduced, approx. 2 minutes.
1¹/₂ cups whipping cream *¹/₂ tbsp. chopped anchovies*	Add and continue cooking on medium heat until slightly thickened, approx. 5 minutes.
1 cup grated provolone cheese (or any soft, mild cheese, i.e. Havarti, brick, etc.) *¹/₂ cup Parmesan*	Add to above sauce, blend well, and purée. Strain sauce, save, and place in large bowl.
4 tbsp. butter	Add to strained sauce and blend well. Add arugula, peppers, pine nuts, and pasta. Combine and serve.

Penne with Tomatoes, Black Olives, and Goat Cheese

*Goat cheese adds a distinct
flavor to this pasta dish.*

Serves 4

¾ lb. penne pasta (short tube)	Cook in boiling water until al dente (firm to the bite). Drain and set aside. Meanwhile, prepare sauce.
1 tbsp. olive oil	Heat in large skillet.
1 garlic clove, crushed / *1 medium onion, chopped*	Add and sauté until onions are soft.
16-oz. can tomatoes, with juice (preferably Italian plum)	Add and cook over low heat, stirring until smooth and thick, approx. 10 minutes. (Break tomatoes with back of spoon.)
salt and pepper to taste / *3 oz. goat cheese, cut into pieces* / *2 oz. black olives (pitted and sliced)* / *sprinkle of chili pepper or fresh chili pepper to taste*	Add to sauce, mix just until cheese has melted. Add pasta and toss.
¼ cup Parmesan cheese	Sprinkle over top and serve.

Per serving (¼th)

Calories:	501
Protein:	19 g
Fat:	15 g
Cholesterol:	26 mg
Carbohydrates:	71 g
Sodium:	778 mg

Fettuccine with Ricotta

*This is a light, simple pasta
with green peas and ricotta cheese.*

Serves 4–5

2 tbsp. olive oil **2 tbsp. butter**	Heat in skillet.
½ medium onion, chopped	Add and sauté until onion is golden.
8 oz. peas (canned or frozen) **salt to taste** **⅛ tsp. dry sage**	Add to onion and cook approx. 5 minutes. Set aside.
¾ cup ricotta cheese **2 egg yolks**	Combine in large bowl.
¾ lb. fettuccine	Cook in boiling water until al dente (firm to the bite). Drain and immediately combine with ricotta mixture and 2 tbsp. hot water.
½ cup grated Parmesan cheese	Add to pasta, combine, and add above onion sauce. Mix well.

Per serving (⅕th)

Calories:	484
Protein:	18 g
Fat:	18 g
Cholesterol:	139 mg
Carbohydrates:	59 g
Sodium:	361 mg

Linguine with Walnut Cheese Sauce

*This mild walnut cheese sauce is
suitable for any pasta or tortellini dish.*

Serves 4

2 egg yolks
½ cup chopped walnuts
3 tbsp. pine nuts
7 oz. mascarpone cheese
(or use cream or ricotta
cheese)
salt to taste
dash of nutmeg

Combine until well mixed and
set aside.

¾ lb. linguine or tagliatelle

Cook in boiling water until al
dente (firm to the bite).

Drain pasta and add sauce
immediately. Serve.

Per serving (¼th)	
Calories:	486
Protein:	19 g
Fat:	15 g
Cholesterol:	153 mg
Carbohydrates:	69 g
Sodium:	139 mg

Bow Tie Pasta with Chicken or Duck and Green Olives
Michela's, Boston

*Fettuccine with
Calamari in a Spicy
Mediterranean
Sauce*
Upstairs at the Pudding,
Boston

Pasta Shells Stuffed with Cheese in a Creamy Tomato Sauce
Umberto al Porto, Vancouver

Pasta Primavera
Giuliano's, Carmel

Fettuccine with Artichokes

Artichokes in a creamy wine sauce.

Serves 4–6

¾ lb. fettuccine	Cook in boiling water until al dente (firm to the bite). Drain and set aside. Meanwhile, prepare sauce.
¼ cup butter	Heat in large skillet.
2 garlic cloves, crushed	Sauté until light brown.
1 (14-oz.) can of artichoke hearts* (drained and quartered) ¼ cup white wine	Add and simmer for 2 minutes.
1¼ cups heavy cream	Add and cook on medium heat until cream begins to bubble, approx. 3 minutes.
salt and pepper to taste	Add along with pasta to above and toss.
½ cup Parmesan cheese	Add and toss until cheese has melted.

*(To cook your own artichokes, see page 15.)

Per serving (⅙th)	
Calories:	486
Protein:	12 g
Fat:	27 g
Cholesterol:	89 mg
Carbohydrates:	48 g
Sodium:	376 mg

Pasta Salad with Roasted Peppers and Onions

*Roasted bell peppers are a delicacy that can
be prepared in minutes for this unusual pasta dish.*

Preheat oven to broil
Serves 4–6

Per serving (⅙th)	
Calories:	445
Protein:	10 g
Fat:	19 g
Cholesterol:	30 mg
Carbohydrates:	58 g
Sodium:	70 mg

¾ lb. small shell pasta or tubes
Cook in boiling water until al dente (firm to the bite). Drain and set aside. Meanwhile, prepare sauce.

6 small bell peppers (any combination of red or yellow)
In the oven under broiler, roast peppers, turning occasionally, just until charred, approx. 10 minutes. Let rest 10 minutes. Rinse under cold water, peel, and remove core and seeds. Slice thinly and reserve.

¼ cup olive oil
Heat in large skillet over high heat.

3 medium onions, sliced salt and pepper
Add and cook until golden brown.

1 tbsp. crushed garlic ¾ tbsp. paprika
Add and cook 1 minute.

3 large tomatoes, diced
Add to above along with sliced peppers, cook 1 more minute. Remove from heat. Add pasta.

1¼ cups sour cream dash of Tabasco (optional)
Add, toss well, and serve.

Pasta with Mushrooms in a Creamy Tomato Sauce

Wild mushrooms such as oyster are wonderful in this light lemon sauce.

Serves 4–5

³/₄ lb. fettuccine	Cook in boiling water until al dente (firm to the bite). Drain and set aside. Meanwhile, prepare sauce.
3 tbsp. butter	Melt butter in large saucepan.
1 lb. sliced mushrooms (preferably wild such as oyster, chanterelle, porcini, etc.) 2 tbsp. crushed garlic	Add and cook for 3 minutes on a medium heat.
1¹/₄ cups heavy cream	Add, turn heat to high, and cook for approx. 3 minutes. Lower heat.
2 tsp. lemon juice ¹/₂ cup diced tomatoes salt and pepper to taste	Add and combine with above. Add pasta and toss.
¹/₃ cup Parmesan cheese	Sprinkle on cheese, toss well, and serve.

Per serving (¹/₅th)

Calories:	567
Protein:	14 g
Fat:	30 g
Cholesterol:	100 mg
Carbohydrates:	59 g
Sodium:	260 mg

Penne with Dried Mushrooms

*Dried mushrooms are a delicacy and well worth the expense. If they are unavailable, try a variety of fresh wild mushrooms. *

Serves 4–6

1 lb. tomatoes (preferably Roma)

Dice and set aside.

*1 oz. dried mushrooms (preferably porcini, but any wild mushroom will do)

Cover with hot water and let stand 20 minutes. Remove from water and slice thinly.

2 tbsp. olive oil

Heat in skillet.

1 medium onion, finely chopped
4 garlic cloves, crushed

Cook in oil until onions are yellow in color. Add drained mushrooms. Cook approx. 3–5 minutes, stirring constantly.

1 small bunch basil leaves, chopped (or 1½ tbsp. dry)
salt and pepper

Add along with diced tomatoes to onion mixture. Cook over medium-low heat, stirring occasionally, for approx. 15 minutes. Partially cover and cook over low heat another 5 minutes until tomatoes become very soft. Let sauce rest approx. 30 minutes, away from heat, in skillet.

1 lb. penne pasta (short tubes)

Cook in boiling water until al dente (firm to the bite). Drain and add to sauce and cook over medium heat for approx. 1 minute.

1 cup heavy cream

Add to pasta and cook until sauce is slightly reduced. Serve.

Per serving (⅙th)
Calories: 477
Protein: 11 g
Fat: 19 g
Cholesterol: 51 mg
Carbohydrates: 64 g
Sodium: 22 mg

Spicy Fettuccine with Sweet Peppers

*The variety of bell peppers, tomatoes,
and spices make this a delicious pasta.*

Serves 4–5

³/₄ lb. fettuccine	Cook in boiling water until firm to the bite (al dente). Drain and set aside. Meanwhile, prepare sauce.
4 small tomatoes (diced)	Set aside.
¹/₂ green pepper **¹/₂ yellow pepper** **¹/₂ red pepper**	Use any combination if these 3 are not available. Slice into ¹/₂″ pieces. Set vegetables aside.
¹/₃ cup olive oil	Heat in skillet.
¹/₂ medium onion, finely chopped **2 crushed garlic cloves** **salt and crushed red pepper to taste**	Add and sauté until onion and garlic turn brown. Increase heat and add tomatoes and sliced peppers. Stir, reduce heat, cover, and simmer approx. 15–20 minutes. Add pasta to sauce and toss.
2 tbsp. butter **³/₄ cup Parmesan cheese**	Add to pasta and serve.

Per serving (¹/₅th)	
Calories:	467
Protein:	14 g
Fat:	21 g
Cholesterol:	22 mg
Carbohydrates:	56 g
Sodium:	320 mg

Penne with Zucchini and Eggplant

*Mozzarella pieces begin to melt over
the pasta and vegetables while being served.*

Serves 4

¾ lb. penne pasta (short tube)	Cook in boiling water until firm to the bite (al dente). Drain and set aside. Meanwhile, prepare sauce.
8 oz. eggplant **7 oz. zucchini**	Cut into sticks.
1 large ripe tomato	Cut into strips (preferably, remove seeds and skin).
5 tbsp. olive oil **1 clove crushed garlic**	Sauté until garlic becomes golden. Add eggplant and zucchini and cook approx. 3 minutes. Add tomato strips.
6 fresh chopped basil leaves (1 tsp. dry) **pepper to taste**	Add and continue to cook for another 2–4 minutes. Add cooked penne to sauce and mix well.
5 oz. mozzarella, cut into small cubes (if possible, smoked cheese tastes best)	Add and sauté until cheese begins to melt. Serve immediately.

Per serving (¼th)

Calories:	593
Protein:	21 g
Fat:	24 g
Cholesterol:	20 mg
Carbohydrates:	73 g
Sodium:	175 mg

Pasta Primavera

*Fresh, crisp vegetables in
a light basil sauce.*

Serves 4–6

¾ lb. linguine	Cook in boiling water until al dente (firm to the bite). Drain and set aside.
1 cup sliced zucchini *1½ cups chopped broccoli* *1½ cups snow peas* *6 asparagus spears, cut into pieces* *1 cup green peas*	Cook in boiling water for 2 minutes. Drain and set aside.
1 tbsp. olive oil *1 medium tomato, diced* *½ tsp. crushed garlic* *¼ cup chopped parsley* *(1 tbsp. dry)* *salt and pepper to taste*	Sauté, just until tomato pieces are soft, approx. 3 minutes. Set aside.
2 tbsp. olive oil *10 sliced mushrooms* *1 tsp. crushed garlic*	Heat oil in large skillet. Sauté mushrooms. When cooked, add above vegetable mixture just long enough to reheat vegetables. Add tomato mixture.
½ cup Parmesan cheese *⅓ cup melted butter* *1 cup heavy cream, warmed* *⅓ cup chopped basil* *(1½ tsp. dry)* *salt and pepper to taste* *⅓ cup pine nuts ** *(preferably toasted)*	Quickly add to above and mix well. Add pasta, toss, and serve.

Per serving (⅙th)

Calories:	680
Protein:	16 g
Fat:	44 g
Cholesterol:	87 mg
Carbohydrates:	58 g
Sodium:	408 mg

*Toast either in oven at 400°F or on top of stove until golden brown.

Pasta with Sun-Dried Tomatoes

*A light sauce enhanced with garlic,
sun-dried tomatoes, and basil.*

Serves 4–6

1 lb. thin pasta (fedilini, spaghettini)	Cook in boiling water until al dente (firm to the bite). Drain and set aside. Meanwhile, prepare sauce.
1 tbsp. olive oil	Heat in skillet.
3 tbsp. crushed garlic	Add and sauté until light brown.
3 cups chopped tomatoes **¾ cup sun-dried tomatoes, thinly sliced** **½ cup chopped basil (1 tbsp. dry)** **½ cup pine nuts ***	Add and cook for 2–3 minutes.
1 cup chicken stock **salt and pepper to taste**	Add to above and cook for another 3 minutes. Add pasta, toss, and serve.

*Toast pine nuts for a better taste either on top of stove or in oven at 400°F.

Per serving (⅙th)

Calories:	442
Protein:	13 g
Fat:	15 g
Cholesterol:	0 mg
Carbohydrates:	67 g
Sodium:	221 mg

Tagliatelle with Mushroom Sauce

*Sweet wine combined with mushrooms
in a light cream sauce.*

Serves 4–6

	1 lb. tagliatelle or fettuccine	Cook in boiling water until al dente (firm to the bite). Drain and set aside. Meanwhile, prepare sauce.
	3 tbsp. butter	Heat in large pan.
	1 shallot or green onion, chopped (white part only), 12 large mushrooms, sliced (preferably wild such as shiitake, oyster, etc.)	Add and sauté until soft. Remove mushroom mixture from pan and set aside.
	4 tbsp. sweet wine (such as Madeira or port)	Add to above pan, increase heat, and cook until almost evaporated.
	6 tbsp. chicken stock	Add and cook for approx. 1 minute.
	1½ cups heavy cream salt and pepper to taste	Add and cook for 3 more minutes on a medium heat. Return mushroom mixture and pasta to pan and blend well. Serve.

Per serving (⅙th)

Calories:	543
Protein:	11 g
Fat:	28 g
Cholesterol:	93 mg
Carbohydrates:	60 g
Sodium:	170 mg

Spaghettini with Sun-Dried Tomatoes and Broccoli

Thin pasta coated with sun-dried tomatoes, garlic, and cheese.

Serves 4–6

¾ lb. spaghettini (or any thin strand pasta)	Cook in boiling water until al dente (firm to the bite). Drain and set aside. Meanwhile, prepare sauce.
2 cups broccoli flowerettes	Blanch in boiling water for 2 minutes. Drain and set aside.
½ cup olive oil 2 tbsp. crushed garlic cloves pinch of crushed chilies (dry or fresh)	In large skillet, add and sauté for 1 minute.
¾ cup sun-dried tomatoes, sliced thin	Add to oil mixture along with broccoli. Sauté for 1 minute. Add pasta and toss.
½ cup Parmesan cheese ½ cup chopped basil (¾ tbsp. dry)	Add to pasta and serve.
⅓ cup toasted pine nuts * as a garnish	

*Toast pine nuts in saucepan or oven at 400°F just until brown.

Per serving (⅙th)	
Calories:	515
Protein:	14 g
Fat:	31 g
Cholesterol:	5 mg
Carbohydrates:	52 g
Sodium:	152 mg

Fettuccine with Artichokes and Mushroom Sauce

Saffron gives this creamy dish a pleasant color and fragrance.

Serves 4–6

1 lb. fettuccine	Cook in boiling water until al dente (firm to the bite). Drain and set aside. Meanwhile, prepare sauce.
10 artichoke hearts * (canned or fresh)	Chop 6 hearts. Save the remainder. (If fresh, sauté in 2 tsp. of butter until soft.) Set aside.
¼ cup vegetable oil **½ lb. chopped mushrooms** **½ tsp. chopped garlic**	Sauté and cook for 5 minutes. Add artichoke hearts.
¼ cup dry white wine	Add to above and cook for 2 minutes.
1½ cups heavy cream	Add and bring to a boil.
½ tsp. chopped saffron (powder or threads) **salt and pepper**	Add and simmer on a low heat for 5 minutes.
⅓ cup Parmesan cheese **parsley, for garnish**	Add to sauce. Add pasta and stir just until mixed. Serve with a garnish of an artichoke heart and a sprinkle of parsley.

*To cook your own artichokes see page 15.

Per serving (⅙th)

Calories:	598
Protein:	14 g
Fat:	32 g
Cholesterol:	79 mg
Carbohydrates:	63 g
Sodium:	229 mg

Fettuccine with Wild Mushrooms

*Dried mushrooms of various varieties
can be found in specialty food stores.
If unavailable use regular mushrooms.*

Serves 2–4

½ lb. fettuccine

Cook in boiling water until al
dente (firm to the bite). Drain
and set aside. Meanwhile,
prepare sauce.

**½ cup dried mushrooms
(preferably porcini)
1 cup hot water**

Let mushrooms soak until soft,
approx. 20–30 minutes.* Drain,
then chop.

4 tbsp. olive oil

Heat in large skillet. Add mushroom pieces and cook for 5
minutes on a medium-low heat.

**¼ cup white wine
salt and pepper
¾ cup heavy cream**

Add and cook for 3 minutes.

¼ cup Parmesan cheese

Add and cook on a low heat for
5 more minutes, or until sauce
gets thick. Add pasta and toss.

Parmesan cheese

Add extra cheese just before
serving.

*If using fresh mushrooms, substitute
½ lb. and do not soak in hot water.

Per serving (¼th)
Calories: 517
Protein: 11 g
Fat: 32 g
Cholesterol: 63 mg
Carbohydrates: 45 g
Sodium: 212 mg

Linguine with Yellow Pepper Sauce

This bright, sweet sauce is best served over black squid pasta. The color contrast is beautiful. Regular pasta still tastes extraordinary with this sauce.

Serves 4–6

1 lb. linguine or fettuccine (preferably black squid pasta, if able to obtain)	Cook in boiling water until al dente (firm to the bite). Drain and set aside. Meanwhile, prepare sauce.
4 tbsp. butter	Melt in large skillet.
2 medium yellow peppers, seeded and cut into slices 2 cloves crushed garlic 1 shallot or green onion, chopped	Add to butter and sauté just until peppers become soft.
1 bay leaf salt and pepper ½ cup chicken stock	Add and simmer for 5 minutes. Purée in a food processor until smooth.
4 tbsp. butter	Add to above purée and blend. Add pasta and toss.

Per serving (⅙th)	
Calories:	439
Protein:	10 g
Fat:	17 g
Cholesterol:	43 mg
Carbohydrates:	60 g
Sodium:	283 mg

Penne with Mushrooms in a Light Cream Sauce

A creamy cheese sauce with mushrooms and green onions.

Serves 4–6

1 lb. penne pasta (short tubes)	Cook in boiling water until al dente (firm to the bite). Drain and set aside. Meanwhile, prepare sauce.
3 tbsp. butter	Heat in large skillet.
1 tbsp. chopped shallots or onions	Sauté for 1 minute.
3 cups chopped mushrooms (preferably mixed such as common, oyster, chanterelle, porcini, etc.)	Add and cook until mushrooms begin to brown, approx. 5 minutes.
1½ cups heavy cream	Add and cook until sauce begins to thicken, approx. 5 minutes.
pinch of chopped parsley	Add along with pasta to sauce and toss.
¼ cup Parmesan cheese black pepper	Add just before serving.

Per serving (⅙th)	
Calories:	564
Protein:	13 g
Fat:	29 g
Cholesterol:	96 mg
Carbohydrates:	62 g
Sodium:	148 mg

Rigatoni with Artichokes

Artichokes in a creamy white wine sauce.

Serves 4–5

³/₄ lb. rigatoni (wide tube pasta)	Cook in boiling water until firm to the bite. Drain and set aside. Meanwhile, prepare sauce.
2 artichoke hearts *	Slice artichokes in pieces. Set aside.
2 tbsp. butter *¹/₂ medium chopped onion*	Heat in large skillet. Add onion and sauté until soft.
3 oz. chopped prosciutto (or ham) *¹/₂ diced carrot*	Add with the artichokes and sauté until carrot is soft.
¹/₂ cup white white	Add and allow to cook until almost all the liquid has evaporated, approx. 2 minutes.
¹/₄ cup chicken broth *²/₃ cup peas*	Add to above and cook until mixture begins to boil.
pepper to taste *1 cup heavy cream*	Add and cook 1-2 more minutes. Add pasta, toss, and serve.

*See page 15 for cooking instructions. If artichokes are not available, substitute another ¹/₂ cup peas.

Per serving (¹/₄th)

Calories:	516
Protein:	13 g
Fat:	24 g
Cholesterol:	80 mg
Carbohydrates:	57 g
Sodium:	393 mg

Rigatoni with Eggplant and Puréed Tomatoes

Eggplant and tomatoes provide a simple sauce over a thick pasta such as rigatoni.

Serves 4–6

¾ lb. rigatoni pasta (wide tube)	Cook in boiling water until firm to the bite (al dente). Drain in cold water and set aside. Meanwhile, prepare sauce.
⅓ cup olive oil	Heat in large skillet.
12 oz. eggplant, cut into cubes	Sauté until eggplant becomes golden, approx. 5 minutes. (If necessary, add more oil.)
28-oz. can tomatoes, with juice (preferably Italian)	Purée and add to eggplant.
salt and pepper	Add to taste and let simmer approx. 15–20 minutes. Add pasta to sauce, toss well.
½ cup Parmesan cheese 2 tbsp. chopped basil (1½ tsp. dry)	Add to pasta and serve.

Per serving (⅙th)

Calories:	400
Protein:	11 g
Fat:	17 g
Cholesterol:	5 mg
Carbohydrates:	51 g
Sodium:	351 mg

Pasta with Spinach Pesto

Serves 4–6 as an appetizer

½ lb. fettuccine	Cook in boiling water until al dente (firm to the bite). Drain and set aside. Meanwhile, prepare sauce.
1 lb. fresh spinach *1 cup water*	Wash spinach and remove stems. In large saucepan, cook spinach in water until wilted, approx. 4 minutes. Drain spinach, squeeze out moisture, and finely chop.
½ tbsp. chopped garlic	Add to spinach. Set aside.
⅓ cup olive oil	Heat in large skillet.
⅓ cup pine nuts	Add and sauté until light brown. Reduce heat to low, add spinach mixture, and cook 3 minutes.
salt and pepper to taste	Add pasta and season.
⅓ cup Parmesan cheese	Add, toss, and serve.

Per serving (⅙th)

Calories:	467
Protein:	9 g
Fat:	36 g
Cholesterol:	58 mg
Carbohydrates:	32 g
Sodium:	156 mg

Spaghetti with Fresh Vegetables and Vodka

A wide array of vegetables with a hint of vodka.

Serves 4–6

¾ lb. spaghetti	Cook in boiling water until al dente (firm to the bite). Drain and set aside. Meanwhile, prepare sauce.
¼ cup olive oil	Heat in large skillet.
2 small carrots, grated *2 small onions, chopped* *1 clove crushed garlic*	Add and sauté until tender.
½ cup white wine *2 medium tomatoes, quartered* *1 small green pepper, diced* *1 medium zucchini, diced*	Add, cover, and cook on a medium heat for approx. 15 minutes.
4 tbsp. chopped parsley (1 tbsp. dry) *salt and pepper to taste* *2 tsp. chopped basil (½ tsp. dry)* *2 tbsp. vodka*	Add and bring mixture to a boil, then simmer uncovered about 10 minutes, until reduced to a thicker consistency.
¼ cup Parmesan cheese	Add pasta and cheese, toss, and serve.

Per serving (⅙th)

Calories:	342
Protein:	10 g
Fat:	11 g
Cholesterol:	2 mg
Carbohydrates:	50 g
Sodium:	114 mg

Bow Ties in Mushroom Tomato Sauce

This is a light tomato sauce that perfectly suits a wide, flat pasta.

Serves 4–5

³/₄ lb. bow tie pasta (farfalle)	Cook in boiling water until al dente (firm to the bite). Drain and set aside.
4 tbsp. butter	Heat in skillet.
3 cups chopped mushrooms (preferably a combination of different varieties)	Add and sauté until golden, approx. 5 minutes.
2 tsp. garlic **2 tbsp. chopped onions or shallots** **pinch of rosemary**	Add to mushrooms and cook just until onions are wilted.
³/₄ cup prepared tomato sauce **³/₄ cup heavy cream**	Add and cook on a medium heat until sauce becomes thicker, approx. 3 minutes.
¹/₃ cup Parmesan cheese	Add to sauce, combine, and add pasta. Stir to combine and serve.

Per serving (¹/₅th)

Calories:	516
Protein:	13 g
Fat:	27 g
Cholesterol:	35 mg
Carbohydrates:	54 g
Sodium:	274 mg

Bow Tie Pasta with Wild Mushrooms

*Any variety of mushrooms will be
delicious in this garlic cheese sauce.*

Serves 4–6

1 lb. bow tie pasta (farfalle or wide noodles)	Cook in boiling water until al dente (firm to the bite). Drain and set aside. Meanwhile, prepare sauce.
6 tbsp. olive oil	Heat in large skillet.
4 crushed garlic cloves	Brown in oil.
12 oz. sliced mushrooms (preferably wild such as porcini or oyster)	Add and sauté until golden, approx. 10 minutes.
4 tbsp. butter **2 cups chicken stock (consommé)** **3 tbsp. chopped parsley (1 tbsp. dry)** **salt and pepper to taste**	Add and cook on medium heat for 5 minutes. Add pasta and mix well.
¾ cup grated Parmesan cheese (or to taste)	Add and mix before serving.

Per serving (⅙th)

Calories:	548
Protein:	15 g
Fat:	28 g
Cholesterol:	101 mg
Carbohydrates:	58 g
Sodium:	625 mg

Fusilli with Artichokes and Tomatoes

Fresh artichokes will make this pasta dish outstanding. But canned will be fine with this garlic tomato sauce.

Serves 4–6

1 lb. fusilli (spiral pasta)	Cook in boiling water until al dente (firm to the bite). Drain and set aside. Meanwhile, prepare sauce.
8 small artichoke hearts* (14-oz. can)	Cut in quarters and set aside.
3 tbsp. olive oil	Heat in large skillet.
2–3 cloves crushed garlic 1 small diced onion	Sauté until onions are tender.
1 (19-oz.) can tomatoes, with juice (preferably Italian plum)	Add along with artichokes and simmer approx. 10 minutes, stirring occasionally to break up tomatoes.
1 small branch of thyme ($^1/_4$ tsp. dry) pepper to taste	Add and cook for 2 minutes. Add pasta and toss.
$^1/_2$ cup Parmesan cheese	Add and serve.

*To cook your own artichokes see page 15.

Per serving (⅙th)	
Calories:	405
Protein:	13 g
Fat:	10 g
Cholesterol:	5 mg
Carbohydrates:	65 g
Sodium:	362 mg

Penne with Mushroom and Onion Sauce

Any variety of mushrooms with this onion purée sauce will be delicious.

Serves 4–6

1 lb. penne pasta (diagonal tubes)	Cook in boiling water until al dente (firm to the bite). Drain and set aside. Meanwhile, prepare sauce.
2 tbsp. olive oil	Heat in large skillet.
3 medium onions, sliced thin salt and pepper	Add and cook until onions are soft. Purée and set aside.
2 tbsp. olive oil 2–3 crushed garlic cloves sprig of rosemary (¹/₂ tsp. dry) 1 lb. sliced mushrooms (preferably wild—shiitake, oyster, etc.) ¹/₂ cup water	Cook in saucepan until mushrooms are tender, approx. 5 minutes. Add onion purée, pasta, and toss.
¹/₂ cup Parmesan cheese garnish with fresh basil	Add before serving.

Per serving (¹/₆th)

Calories:	439
Protein:	14 g
Fat:	12 g
Cholesterol:	5 mg
Carbohydrates:	67 g
Sodium:	163 mg

Linguine with Chick Pea Sauce

*This unusual sauce works
well over thin pasta.*

Serves 4–6

¾ *lb. linguine*	Cook in boiling water until al dente (firm to the bite). Drain and set aside. Meanwhile, prepare sauce.
3 tbsp. olive oil	Heat in saucepan.
3 cloves crushed garlic *4 sage leaves (¼ tsp. dry)* *pinch fresh rosemary* *(⅛ tsp. dry)* *hot pepper to taste*	Add and sauté for 1 minute.
2 cups chicken stock *2 tbsp. tomato paste*	Add and cook on a medium-high heat for 5 minutes.
12 oz. chick peas (drained)	Add and cook for another 10–12 minutes. Purée and toss with pasta. Add some extra olive oil before serving, if pasta appears too dry.

Per serving (⅙th)
Calories: 373
Protein: 12 g
Fat: 9 g
Cholesterol: 3 mg
Carbohydrates: 60 g
Sodium: 324 mg

Egg Noodles with Mushrooms in Red Wine Sauce

The dried mushrooms are a delicacy in this garlic tomato sauce.

Serves 4–6

1 lb. flat egg noodles (or fettuccine)	Cook in boiling water until firm to the bite (al dente). Drain and set aside.
½ cup dry mushrooms * (preferably wild) **½ cup red wine**	Soak mushrooms in 1 cup of hot water just until soft, approx. 20 minutes. Drain. Bring wine to a boil, add mushrooms, and cook for 2 minutes. Drain, reserve wine, cool, then chop mushrooms. Set aside.
2 tbsp. olive oil **½ onion, chopped** **1 tsp. crushed garlic**	In a large skillet, sauté until onions are light brown.
½ cup chopped bacon (preferably Italian pancetta)	Add and sauté until light brown. (Do not drain.)
½ cup white chopped mushrooms	Add along with above dry mushrooms and sauté until mushrooms turn golden, approx. 5 minutes.
1¼ lb. puréed tomatoes (canned or fresh) **½ cup consommé (chicken or beef)**	Add to above along with reserved red wine. Simmer until thick, approx. 30–40 minutes. Add pasta, toss, and serve.

*Dry mushrooms are available in specialty food stores. If unavailable, substitute ½ lb. fresh mushrooms of any variety. Do not soak fresh mushrooms.

Per serving (⅙th)

Calories:	418
Protein:	12 g
Fat:	14 g
Cholesterol:	79 mg
Carbohydrates:	58 g
Sodium:	193 mg

Pasta with Meat or Poultry

Linguine with Spicy Sausage

A simple thin pasta coated with morsels of Italian spicy sausage.

Serves 4–5

¾ lb. linguine	Cook in boiling water until al dente (firm to the bite). Drain and set aside. Meanwhile, prepare sauce.
4 tbsp. olive oil *¾ lb. sausage (medium to spicy)*	Remove skin from sausage, chop and add with oil to large skillet. Sauté until nearly done, approx. 5 minutes.
Sprinkle hot red chili pepper (dry or fresh) to taste *12 chopped basil leaves (2 tsp. dry)* *salt and pepper to taste*	Add and simmer 2 minutes. Add pasta to skillet and toss. Add a little more oil if pasta appears too dry.
4–6 tbsp. Parmesan cheese *1 tbsp. chopped parsley*	Sprinkle on pasta and serve.

Per serving (⅕th)	
Calories:	648
Protein:	17 g
Fat:	40 g
Cholesterol:	48 mg
Carbohydrates:	52 g
Sodium:	562 mg

Macaroni with Chicken and Sun-Dried Tomatoes

Small shells of pasta and chicken coated with a creamy, garlic tomato sauce.

Serves 4–6

³/₄ lb. macaroni	Cook in boiling water until firm to the bite (al dente). Drain and set aside. Meanwhile, prepare sauce.
1 cup diced, cooked chicken (smoked or roasted preferred) *3 tbsp. chopped sun-dried tomatoes* *1¹/₄ cups heavy cream* *2 tsp. chopped garlic*	Combine and bring to a boil and cook for approx. 5 minutes over a low heat.
4 tbsp. butter *¹/₄ cup Parmesan cheese*	Stir into above and remove from heat.
salt and pepper *dash of nutmeg*	Add to above, add macaroni, and stir. Serve.

Per serving (¹/₆th)

Calories:	486
Protein:	14 g
Fat:	28 g
Cholesterol:	98 mg
Carbohydrates:	44 g
Sodium:	299 mg

Linguine with Italian Sausage and Red Wine Sauce

A thick tomato wine sauce with spicy sausage pieces.

Serves 4–6

¾ **lb. linguine or thin strand pasta**	Cook in boiling water until al dente (firm to the bite). Drain and set aside. Meanwhile, prepare sauce.
2 **tbsp. butter** 1 **tbsp. olive oil**	Heat in skillet.
1 **medium onion, chopped**	Add and sauté until soft.
¾ **lb. Italian sausage (medium spicy)**	Remove skin, chop, and add to above. Cook until done, stirring continuously, approx. 5 minutes.
¾ **cup red wine** 2 **cups (prepared) tomato sauce** **salt and pepper to taste** 2 **tbsp. butter**	Add to above sauce. Cook over low heat approx. 10 minutes, until thick. Add pasta and toss well. Sauté an additional 2 minutes.
¼ **cup Parmesan cheese**	Sprinkle on pasta and serve.

Per serving (⅙th)	
Calories:	588
Protein:	16 g
Fat:	34 g
Cholesterol:	64 mg
Carbohydrates:	48 g
Sodium:	739 mg

Fettuccine with Bacon and Fresh Vegetables

Crisp bacon with crisp vegetables in a creamy cheese sauce.

Serves 4–6

³⁄₄ lb. fettuccine	Cook in boiling water until al dente (firm to the bite). Drain and set aside. Meanwhile, prepare sauce.
2 tbsp. olive oil *4 oz. chopped bacon* *(preferably Italian* *pancetta)*	Sauté until bacon becomes crispy, approx. 5 minutes. (Do not drain off oil.)
²⁄₃ cup chopped broccoli *²⁄₃ cup chopped mushrooms* *²⁄₃ cup chopped tomatoes* *¹⁄₃ cup chopped carrots*	Add and sauté for approx. 5 minutes.
1 cup heavy cream *4 tbsp. Parmesan cheese* *1 tbsp. butter* *salt and pepper to taste*	Add and stir into a creamy sauce, about 2 minutes. Add pasta, toss, and serve.

Per serving (¹⁄₆th)

Calories:	558
Protein:	11 g
Fat:	36 g
Cholesterol:	70 mg
Carbohydrates:	47 g
Sodium:	264 mg

Whole Red Peppers Stuffed with Capellini and Prosciutto Ham*

A beautiful meal with the capellini spilling out of the bright red peppers. Perfect as an appetizer or side dish.

Preheat oven to broil
Serves 6

Per serving (1/6th)	
Calories:	361
Protein:	10 g
Fat:	13 g
Cholesterol:	27 mg
Carbohydrates:	49 g
Sodium:	457 mg

6 whole red peppers (or yellow peppers work well)

Broil in oven or grill approx. 10 minutes or until charred, turning often. Let cool for 5 minutes. Remove top and save, peel skin, and de-seed, leaving whole pepper intact. (You can do this under cool running water.)

¾ lb. thin pasta (capellini, spaghettini, etc.)

Cook in boiling water until al dente (firm to the bite). Drain and set aside.

1 tbsp. olive oil
1 tsp. crushed garlic

Heat olive oil in large skillet. Sauté garlic lightly.

1 large tomato, chopped
pepper to taste
1¼ cups chicken stock
3 basil leaves (1 tsp. dry)
4 tbsp. butter

Add tomato, pepper, and stock and cook over high heat for approx. 3 minutes. Lower heat. Add basil and butter and stir to make a creamy sauce.

4 slices prosciutto (or ham), cut in strips

Add to above along with pasta. Toss and fill peppers with as much as can fit. Save remainder as a side dish. Replace pepper top over pasta.

Parmesan or Romano cheese

Serve with pasta.

*This pasta dish can be served on its own without the red peppers.

Spaghetti with Chicken Livers

Morsels of chicken livers
tossed with spaghetti and tomatoes.

Serves 4–5

³/₄ lb. spaghetti	Cook in boiling water until al dente (firm to the bite). Drain and set aside. Meanwhile, prepare sauce.
2 tbsp. butter *3 tbsp. oil*	Heat in large skillet.
1 small onion, chopped	Sauté until onion is golden.
6 chicken livers, cut into small cubes	Add and sauté for a minute.
14-oz. can tomatoes, with juice (preferably Italian) *3 basil leaves or ¹/₂ tsp. dry* *salt and pepper*	Add and cook on a medium heat for 15 minutes, until tomatoes are well-combined, stirring often. Add pasta and toss.
¹/₄ cup Parmesan cheese	Sprinkle over pasta and mix well. Serve immediately.

Per serving (⅕th)

Calories:	429
Protein:	14 g
Fat:	15 g
Cholesterol:	67 mg
Carbohydrates:	56 g
Sodium:	304 mg

Fusilli with Bacon
and Radicchio Lettuce

*Radicchio along with bacon goes
beautifully with tomatoes and cheese.*

Serves 4–6

1 lb. fusilli (spiral pasta)	Cook in boiling water until al dente (firm to the bite). Drain and set aside. Meanwhile, prepare sauce.
1 tsp. oil **¼ lb. diced bacon** **(preferably Italian pancetta)**	In large skillet, add and sauté until bacon becomes limp. Either keep or pour off oil.
½ cup finely chopped onions **1 tsp. crushed garlic cloves**	Add and continue to sauté briefly.
1 medium head of radicchio, * cut into wedges	Add and cook on a medium heat until wilted, approx. 5 minutes.
1 cup white wine	Add and cook to reduce slightly, approx. 3 minutes.
4 cups coarsely chopped tomatoes **2 tbsp. tomato paste**	Add and simmer for 10 minutes, stirring occasionally.
salt and pepper to taste **2 tbsp. olive oil**	Add and combine. Add pasta and combine well.
¼ lb. mozzarella cheese, diced	Top pasta with cheese and serve.

*Radicchio is a small head of red lettuce with a slightly bitter taste. Available in vegetable section of supermarket.

Per serving (⅙th)	
Calories:	540
Protein:	17 g
Fat:	22 g
Cholesterol:	26 mg
Carbohydrates:	65 g
Sodium:	306 mg

Shell Pasta with Sweet Sausage

Delicate pasta shells in a creamy sauce with sweet sausage.

Serves 2–4

¹/₂ lb. small shell pasta or macaroni

Cook in boiling water until firm to the bite (al dente). Drain and set aside. Meanwhile, prepare sauce.

6 oz. sweet Italian sausage (mild)
1 tbsp. olive oil

Remove skin, chop, and sauté in oil until done, breaking with a fork to crumble. Set aside.

¹/₂ cup heavy cream
¹/₂ cup half and half (or milk)

Bring to a boil.

pinch of nutmeg and pepper
¹/₃ cup Parmesan cheese
1 tbsp. chopped parsley

Add to above along with cooked sausage and heat thoroughly. Add pasta to sauce, toss, and serve with more Parmesan cheese if desired.

Per serving (¹/₄th)
Calories: 578
Protein: 17 g
Fat: 36 g
Cholesterol: 80 mg
Carbohydrates: 46 g
Sodium: 449 mg

Fusilli with Sausages and Mushrooms

*A creamy tomato sauce spiced up
with pieces of Italian sausage.*

*Serves 6–8
as an appetizer*

1 lb. fusilli (twisted pasta)	Cook in boiling water until al dente (firm to the bite). Drain and set aside. Meanwhile, prepare sauce.
3 tbsp. oil	Heat in large skillet.
¾ lb. Italian sausage (as spicy as desired)	Remove skin. Sauté sausage in oil and crush with a fork, until cooked. Set aside.
1 medium onion, finely chopped 2 tbsp. oil	In another pan, sauté until golden.
4 oz. chopped mushrooms	Add to onions and sauté until soft. Mix with sausages and sauté for 2 minutes.
4 tbsp. dry white wine 1 tbsp. butter 1 tsp. chopped parsley ½ cup prepared tomato sauce	Add to above and mix well.
1½ cups heavy cream	Add to above and simmer at a low heat for approx. 20–30 minutes, stirring frequently, until thicker. Add pasta to sauce.
¾ cup Parmesan cheese	Add to above, mix quickly, and serve.

Per serving (⅛th)

Calories:	668
Protein:	16 g
Fat:	45 g
Cholesterol:	96 mg
Carbohydrates:	47 g
Sodium:	466 mg

Spaghetti with Sausages and Tomatoes

Spicy sausage pieces in a tomato wine sauce.

Serves 4–6

¾ lb. spaghetti	Cook in boiling water until al dente (firm to the bite). Drain and set aside. Meanwhile, prepare sauce.
4 tbsp. olive oil	Heat in large pan.
1 medium red onion, finely chopped	Add and cook on a moderate heat until soft.
6 oz. sausage (medium spicy)	Remove skin, chop, and add to above and cook for approx. 5 minutes, breaking sausage with a fork, until cooked.
3 small tomatoes, cubed *3 basil leaves (½ tsp. dry)* *salt to taste* *dash of red pepper* *½ cup red wine*	Add to above and cook 10 more minutes, stirring often, until sauce thickens.
¼ cup Parmesan cheese	Add along with pasta, toss, and serve.

Per serving (⅙th)

Calories:	438
Protein:	12 g
Fat:	22 g
Cholesterol:	21 mg
Carbohydrates:	46 g
Sodium:	289 mg

Fettuccine with Cheese, Tomatoes, and Italian Sausage

The melting mozzarella is mouth watering when served over this spicy tomato sauce.

Serves 2–4

¹/₂ lb. fettuccine	Cook in boiling water until firm to the bite (al dente). Drain and set aside.
6 oz. skinned and diced medium spiced Italian sausage	Cook until done in a fry pan. Set aside.
2 tbsp. butter *1 tsp. garlic, chopped*	Heat in large saucepan and cook garlic until lightly browned.
¹/₃ cup white wine *12 oz. diced tomatoes (preferably Italian plum)* *10 leaves of fresh chopped basil (¹/₂ tbsp. dry)* *salt and pepper to taste*	Add ingredients and simmer for 5 minutes.
1 tbsp. grated Romano or Parmesan cheese	Add along with cooked sausage to tomato mixture. Toss with fettuccine until well-mixed. Pour into serving bowl.
4 oz. finely diced mozzarella cheese	Add to fettuccine, toss lightly, and serve.

Per serving (¼th)

Calories:	542
Protein:	20 g
Fat:	29 g
Cholesterol:	62 mg
Carbohydrates:	48 g
Sodium:	560 mg

Linguine with Chicken, Mushrooms, and Sun-Dried Tomatoes

Sun-dried tomatoes and mushrooms in a garlic wine sauce.

Serves 4

³/₄ lb. linguine (preferably whole wheat) — Cook in boiling water until al dente (firm to the bite). Drain and set aside. Meanwhile, prepare sauce.

**3 tbsp. olive oil
2 tsp. crushed garlic** — Heat in large saucepan for 1 minute.

12 oz. raw chicken breast, cut into small pieces (flour for dusting) — Coat in flour and add to hot oil. Sauté just until slightly undercooked.

**4 tbsp. white wine
2 tbsp. chopped green onions or scallions
1 oz. sun-dried tomatoes, chopped
8 large mushrooms, chopped (preferably wild such as oyster or shiitake)
2 cups chicken stock** — Add and simmer approx. 5 minutes. Add pasta, toss, and serve.

Per serving (¹/₄th)

Calories:	529
Protein:	33 g
Fat:	12 g
Cholesterol:	52 mg
Carbohydrates:	68 g
Sodium:	536 mg

Linguine with Lychees, Chicken, and Cashews

Resembles a Chinese dish in a light, creamy tomato sauce.

Serves 4–6

1 lb. linguine	Cook in boiling water until al dente (firm to the bite). Drain and set aside. Meanwhile, prepare sauce.
2 tbsp. butter	Heat in large skillet.
8 oz. cubed cooked chicken (preferably smoked or roasted) **4 oz. canned lychees * (drained and chopped)**	Add and cook on a medium-high heat until chicken begins to brown, approx. 3–5 minutes.
1 cup heavy cream **1 cup prepared tomato sauce**	Add to above and cook for approx. 5 minutes. Add linguine and toss.
¹/₃ cup chopped cashew nuts **¹/₃ cup chopped green onions**	Garnish pasta with nuts and onions.
¹/₄ cup Parmesan cheese **black pepper**	Serve immediately with pepper and cheese.

*Lychees are a Chinese fruit available in cans in the Chinese area of a supermarket.

Per serving (¹/₆th)

Calories:	584
Protein:	21 g
Fat:	26 g
Cholesterol:	88 mg
Carbohydrates:	64 g
Sodium:	360 mg

Fettuccine with Beef Tenderloin and Chicken

*This resembles a Japanese dinner with
tender morsels of beef and chicken.*

Serves 4–6

1 lb. fettuccine	Cook in boiling water until al dente (firm to the bite). Drain and set aside. Meanwhile, prepare sauce.	
2 tbsp. olive oil	Heat in large skillet.	
6 oz. sliced beef tenderloin (raw) **6 oz. sliced chicken breast (raw)** **4 tbsp. finely chopped ginger (preferably gari or sushi pickled ginger, available in specialty section of supermarket)**	Add and sauté until meat is just cooked. Remove beef and chicken. Leave pan on a medium-high heat.	
1 tsp. chopped garlic **2 tbsp. chopped basil (1/2 tsp. dry)**	Add to hot pan.	
1 1/2 cups heavy cream	Add to above and allow sauce to simmer approx. 5 minutes. Return meat to pan. Add fettuccine and toss.	
1/4 cup Parmesan cheese **black pepper**	Serve with cheese and black pepper.	

Per serving (1/6th)

Calories: 613

Protein: 25 g

Fat: 29 g

Cholesterol: 111 mg

Carbohydrates: 59 g

Sodium: 119 mg

Penne with Mushrooms and Chicken (or Duck)

The chef suggests using duck meat with this mushroom-based creamy garlic sauce, but chicken is a delicious second choice.

Serves 4–5
as an appetizer

8 oz. penne pasta (short tube)	Cook in boiling water until al dente (firm to the bite). Drain and set aside. Meanwhile, prepare sauce.
2 tbsp. butter **2 tbsp. olive oil**	Melt in skillet.
2 crushed garlic cloves **1 medium sweet onion, diced** **1 tbsp. chopped basil ($^1/_2$ tsp. dry)** **1 tbsp. chopped parsley (1 tsp. dry)**	Add and cook until onions are soft.
$^1/_4$ cup white wine	Add and cook on a medium heat for approx. 2 minutes.
$^1/_4$ cup chicken stock	Add and cook for approx. 2 minutes.
$^1/_2$ cup heavy cream	Add and simmer about 5 minutes. Set mixture aside.
2 tbsp. butter **2 tbsp. olive oil**	Melt in large skillet.

(continued)

Per serving (¹⁄₄th)

Calories:	517
Protein:	14 g
Fat:	31g
Cholesterol:	72 mg
Carbohydrates:	41 g
Sodium:	375 mg

Penne with Mushrooms and Chicken (or Duck) *(continued)*

4 oz. cooked chicken or duck, sliced (preferably smoked) *1 tomato, chopped* *¼ lb. chopped mushrooms (preferably a combination of a variety of mushrooms)* *1 small bunch arugula, chopped*	Add these ingredients and sauté for 2–3 minutes. Add above cream sauce and cook on a low heat for approx. 5 minutes. Add pasta and toss.
⅓ cup Parmesan cheese	Sprinkle and serve.

Bow Tie Pasta with Chicken or Duck and Green Olives

The chef recommends that duck is best with this spicy sauce, but chicken is fine.

Serves 4–5

¾ lb. bow tie pasta (farfalle) or wide flat pasta	Cook in boiling water until al dente (firm to the bite). Drain and set aside. Meanwhile, prepare sauce.
3 oz. diced bacon (preferably Italian pancetta) *3 oz. spicy sausage, skinned and chopped* *¼ small bunch rosemary, chopped (½ tsp. dry)*	Sauté ingredients in large skillet. (Either pour off oil or keep.)
¼ small bunch sage, chopped (½ tsp. dry) *3 cloves garlic, chopped* *15 sliced medium green olives, pitted* *dash of red pepper flakes to taste*	Add and sauté for 2 minutes.
juice from ¼ lemon *1½ cups chicken stock*	Add and simmer approx. 5 minutes.
1 tbsp. cornstarch dissolved in 1 tbsp. cold water	Add to sauce to thicken and cook for approx. 2 minutes.
6 oz. cooked chicken or duck meat, sliced thinly *salt and pepper to taste*	Add and combine. Add pasta and toss. Serve.

Per serving (⅕th)

Calories:	516
Protein:	20 g
Fat:	24 g
Cholesterol:	108 mg
Carbohydrates:	52 g
Sodium:	1195 mg

Spaghetti with Chicken and Broccoli

Broccoli and chicken morsels
in a tomato garlic sauce.

Serves 4–6

¾ lb. spaghetti	Cook in boiling water until al dente (firm to the bite). Drain and set aside. Meanwhile, prepare sauce.
1 medium head broccoli florets	Cook in boiling water for 2 minutes. Drain and set aside.
1½ tbsp. oil	Heat in large skillet.
12 oz. raw chicken breasts, cubed **salt and pepper** **2 tsp. crushed garlic** **2 small tomatoes, diced** **(preferably Italian plum)**	Add and sauté along with above broccoli just until chicken is still slightly undercooked, approx. 5–8 minutes.
⅔ cup chicken stock	Add to above and cook on a medium heat for 2–3 minutes until sauce thickens.
1 tbsp. butter	Add to above along with pasta and toss. Serve.

Per serving (⅙th)	
Calories:	354
Protein:	23 g
Fat:	7 g
Cholesterol:	38 mg
Carbohydrates:	49 g
Sodium:	219 mg

Fettuccine with Venison Bolognese

Venison is a hearty, gamy meat with a distinct flavor. It is delicious in this wine and light cream sauce. If you cannot find venison, use beef instead.

Serves 4–6

1 lb. fettuccine or tagliatelle	Cook in boiling water until al dente (firm to the bite). Drain and set aside.
¼ cup olive oil **2 tbsp. butter**	Heat in large saucepan.
4 crushed garlic cloves	Add and cook for 1 minute.
3 tbsp. finely chopped onion **3 tbsp. finely chopped carrot** **3 tbsp. finely chopped celery**	Add and cook on a medium heat until vegetables become soft.
8 oz. ground beef **8 oz. ground venison**	Add and break up meat with a spoon. Cook until lightly browned. (Pour off fat if desired.)
½ cup red wine **½ cup white wine**	Turn up heat, add, and cook for approx. 3 minutes.
½ cup light cream **pinch of nutmeg**	Add and cook for another 3 minutes.
1 (28-oz. can) tomatoes, without juice (preferably Italian plum) **salt and pepper to taste**	Add, breaking up while stirring. Turn down heat and simmer approx. 1½ hours. Add pasta and toss. (If using venison, allow to cook longer, until tender.)
¼ cup Parmesan or to taste	Sprinkle on before serving.

Per serving (⅙th)

Calories: 665

Protein: 29 g

Fat: 31 g

Cholesterol: 92 mg

Carbohydrates: 65 g

Sodium: 379 mg

Tagliatelle Carbonara

*A light egg and cheese sauce
with diced bacon.*

Serves 4–5

¾ lb. tagliatelle or fettuccine	Cook in boiling water until al dente (firm to the bite). Drain and set aside. Meanwhile, prepare sauce.
6 eggs *⅓ cup Parmesan cheese* *¼ cup heavy cream* *⅛ cup chopped parsley* *(1 tbsp. dry)* *salt and pepper to taste*	Whisk together and set aside.
2 tbsp. butter	Melt in large saucepan.
½ cup diced bacon *(preferably Italian pancetta)* *1 medium onion, diced*	Add and cook until bacon is lightly colored and onion is clear, approx. 5 minutes. (Drain off excess fat from pan if desired.)
	Add pasta and mix over low heat for a few seconds. Add egg mixture and stir slowly until egg has thickened, not scrambled.
	Serve immediately with more Parmesan cheese if desired.

Per serving (⅕th)

Calories:	542
Protein:	20 g
Fat:	26 g
Cholesterol:	370 mg
Carbohydrates:	54 g
Sodium:	392 mg

Spaghetti with Chicken Livers and Prosciutto

Chicken liver and prosciutto pieces in a buttery sauce.

Serves 4–6

¾ lb. spaghetti	Cook in boiling water until al dente (firm to the bite). Drain and set aside. Meanwhile, prepare sauce.
3 tbsp. butter *3 tbsp. olive oil*	Heat in large skillet.
12 oz. chicken livers, halved	Add and sauté just until done.
salt and pepper *6 oz. thinly sliced ham,* *cut into small pieces* *(preferably prosciutto)*	Add and blend. Add spaghetti.
3 tbsp. Parmesan cheese *3 tbsp. butter*	Add to above and toss.

Per serving (⅙th)	
Calories:	532
Protein:	27 g
Fat:	27 g
Cholesterol:	403 mg
Carbohydrates:	43 g
Sodium:	581 mg

Fettuccine with Prosciutto and Green Peas

A cheese egg sauce over fettuccine is delicious with chopped ham.

Serves 4

³/₄ lb. fettuccine	Cook in boiling water until al dente (firm to the bite). Drain and set aside. Meanwhile, prepare sauce.
1 cup green peas (fresh or frozen) *¹/₂ cup chicken broth*	Simmer in saucepan until tender. Set aside.
3 tbsp. butter	Melt in saucepan.
1 small onion, chopped	Add and sauté until golden brown.
¹/₄ lb. chopped prosciutto or ham	Add to above along with peas and broth. Cook for 1 minute. Set aside.
2 large eggs *¹/₃ cup Parmesan cheese*	Beat in large bowl. Add the pasta and above ham mixture. Stir until well-mixed.
Parmesan cheese	Add extra cheese before serving.

Per serving (¹/₄th)

Calories:	571
Protein:	24 g
Fat:	19 g
Cholesterol:	180 mg
Carbohydrates:	71 g
Sodium:	859 mg

Pasta with Chicken and Fiddleheads in a Garlic Cream Sauce

If possible, try to obtain red pepper pasta and smoked or roasted chicken. The cream sauce is delicate and sweet.

*Serves 4–6
as an appetizer*

¾ lb. pasta (preferably red pepper pasta)	Cook in boiling water until firm to the bite (al dente). Drain and set aside.
1 tbsp. butter	Melt in saucepan.
¼ cup minced shallots or onions **1 bay leaf** **2 tsp. minced garlic**	Add and sauté for 1 minute.
¼ cup white wine **1 cup chicken stock** **1 cup heavy cream** **1 sprig rosemary**	Add wine and cook for 1 minute, or until reduced to half. Add stock and cook for approx. 3 minutes, or until reduced to half. Add cream and rosemary to above and cook for 2 minutes on medium heat. Set aside.
12 oz. cooked diced chicken (preferably smoked or roasted)	Set aside.
½ lb. fiddleheads * **1 tbsp. butter**	Wash well and sauté in butter for about 3 minutes. Set aside.
	Combine pasta, sauce, chicken, and fiddleheads. Toss well and serve.

*A vegetable available in specialty fruit markets. If unavailable fresh, buy canned.

Per serving (⅙th)

Calories:	654
Protein:	46 g
Fat:	30 g
Cholesterol:	162 mg
Carbohydrates:	45 g
Sodium:	1036 mg

Pasta with Seafood

Thin Pasta with Shrimp, Red Peppers, and Pine Nuts

A light pasta dish with a garlic wine sauce coated with pine nuts, red peppers, and shrimp.

Serves 2–4

½ lb. linguine or tagliolini	Cook in boiling water until al dente (firm to the bite). Drain and set aside. Meanwhile, prepare sauce.
¾ cup white wine **¼ cup chopped onions or shallots**	Boil approx. 5 minutes. Remove from heat.
4 tbsp. butter	Whisk into above slowly, until all is incorporated. (Keep warm and set aside.)
2 tbsp. olive oil	Heat in skillet.
8 oz. medium shrimps (peeled and deveined) **⅓ cup toasted pine nuts *** **1 large garlic clove, crushed** **1 large red pepper, sliced thin**	Add ingredients and sauté just until shrimps turn pink, about 2 minutes. Set aside. Add pasta to shrimp mixture along with wine mixture and toss well.
1 tbsp. chopped oregano **(½ tsp. dry)** **1 tbsp. chopped basil** **(½ tsp. dry)** **1 tbsp. chopped parsley**	Sprinkle over pasta, toss, and serve.

Per serving (¼th)

Calories:	606
Protein:	24 g
Fat:	34 g
Cholesterol:	118 mg
Carbohydrates:	52 g
Sodium:	221 mg

*Toast either in oven at 400°F just until golden or on top of stove in skillet.

Thin Pasta with Scallops

The combination of black and white pasta makes this an elegant dish.

Serves 4

³/₄ lb. thin pasta (tagliolini, linguine) (preferably use half white pasta and half black* (squid) pasta.

Cook in boiling water until al dente (firm to the bite). Drain and set aside. Meanwhile, prepare sauce.

1 cup heavy cream
1 cup fish stock (or clam juice)

Combine and bring to a boil. Simmer for approx. 10 minutes. Increase heat to medium.

1 tbsp. cornstarch or arrowroot
¹/₄ cup water

Dissolve cornstarch in water and add a small amount at a time to cream mixture, cooking just until mixture thickens to coat the back of a spoon.

¹/₂ tsp. saffron powder or threads**
³/₄ lb. scallops (preferably bay)

Add to above and simmer for approx. 3–5 minutes, just until scallops are cooked. (Do not overcook.)

Add pasta, toss, and serve.

*Black pasta (squid ink pasta) is available at specialty pasta stores.
**A spice available at specialty food stores.

Per serving (¹/₄th)	
Calories:	614
Protein:	31 g
Fat:	23 g
Cholesterol:	122 mg
Carbohydrates:	70 g
Sodium:	302 mg

Salmon Fettuccine

*Undercook the salmon just a
bit to make this pasta perfect.*

Serves 4–5

¾ **lb. fettuccine**	Cook in boiling water until firm to the bite (al dente). Drain and set aside. Meanwhile, prepare sauce.
4 tbsp. butter **1 tbsp. olive oil**	Heat in large skillet.
1 celery stalk, sliced thin **1 carrot, sliced thin** **3 cloves crushed garlic**	Sauté until vegetables become very soft.
¾ **lb. salmon fillets,** **skinned, boned, and** **cut into cubes**	Add to vegetables and cook over low heat for approx. 3 minutes. Do not let salmon overcook.
½ **cup white wine** **(preferably sparkling)** **salt and pepper to taste**	Cover and cook over low heat for approx. 5 minutes, until sauce reduces.
1 cup tomato sauce ½ **cup half and half** **(light cream)**	Add, cook over low heat for approx. 2 minutes. Add pasta to sauce, mix gently, and serve.

Per serving (⅕th)	
Calories:	533
Protein:	28 g
Fat:	20 g
Cholesterol:	67 mg
Carbohydrates:	55 g
Sodium:	303 mg

Linguine with Shrimp and Clams (or Mussels)

Seafood in a garlic wine sauce is best served over black squid pasta, but it will be delicious over regular as well.

Serves 4–6

1 lb. linguine (preferably black pasta)	Cook in boiling water until firm to the bite (al dente). Drain, set aside.
12 medium shrimp, peeled and deveined	Boil in a small amount of water just until pink, drain, and cut into small pieces. Set aside.
10 asparagus spears	Cut into small pieces and place in boiling water for 1 minute. Drain and set aside.
3 tbsp. olive oil **1 crushed garlic clove**	Heat oil in pan. Add garlic and sauté until golden.
1 lb. fresh clams (or mussels) **³/₄ cup water or white wine**	Add and boil for 5 minutes or until shells open. Reserve seafood and set aside. (Discard shells.)
2 tbsp. olive oil **1 small carrot, diced** **1 celery stalk, diced** **2 green onions, chopped** **³/₄ cup white wine** **6 tbsp. cream**	Heat oil in pan. Add vegetables and cook for 3 minutes. Add wine and cream to vegetables and cook on a medium heat for 3–4 minutes.
6 tbsp. butter	Add to above, mix, and then purée in food processor. Strain, reserving sauce. Add shrimp, asparagus tips, and clams or mussels to sauce and mix well. Toss with pasta and serve.

Per serving (⅙th)	
Calories:	619
Protein:	18 g
Fat:	30 g
Cholesterol:	91 mg
Carbohydrates:	61 g
Sodium:	191 mg

Fettuccine with Monkfish

Monkfish, considered imitation lobster, in a vodka-based cream sauce.

Serves 4–6

¾ lb. fettuccine	Cook in boiling water until al dente (firm to the bite). Drain and set aside. Meanwhile, prepare sauce.
1½ cups heavy cream **grated rind from ½ large lemon** **¼ cup chopped basil leaves (1 tsp. dry)**	Heat just until hot. Set aside.
2 tbsp. melted butter **1 lb. monkfish, *** **cut into 2″ pieces**	In large skillet, sauté over medium heat until just barely cooked, approx. 5 minutes. Remove fish pieces from pan. Set fish aside.
3 tbsp. vodka	Add to pan juices along with above cream mixture. Stir over high heat for approx. 4 minutes. Add fish pieces and simmer approx. 5 minutes.
2 oz. thinly sliced prosciutto or ham **¼ cup Parmesan cheese**	Add to above and then add pasta. Toss well and serve.

*If monkfish or lobster is not available, substitute a firm white fish.

Per serving (⅙th)

Calories:	558
Protein:	28 g
Fat:	28 g
Cholesterol:	200 mg
Carbohydrates:	45 g
Sodium:	338 mg

Fettuccine with Scallops and Smoked Salmon

A hint of sour cream with scallops and smoked salmon in a creamy cheese sauce.

Serves 4–6

¾ lb. fettuccine (or green pasta if possible)	Cook in boiling water until al dente (firm to the bite). Drain and set aside. Meanwhile, prepare sauce.
3 tbsp. butter	Heat in large skillet.
1 lb. scallops 2 tbsp. crushed garlic	Sauté in pan for approx. 2 minutes, or just until scallops are barely cooked.
1¼ cups heavy cream 2 tbsp. sour cream	Add to above and bring to a boil. Turn heat off. Do not overcook scallops.
1 cup mixture of Parmesan and Romano cheese (or all Parmesan if desired) * 4 oz. smoked salmon, chopped	Add to above, mix well, and add pasta. Toss and serve.

Garnish with fish roe (caviar).

*Romano cheese is a sharp, salty cheese. Use all Parmesan if a milder taste is desired.

Per serving (⅙th)	
Calories:	612
Protein:	35 g
Fat:	31 g
Cholesterol:	141 mg
Carbohydrates:	48 g
Sodium:	1723 mg

Linguine with Mixed Seafood

*Any combination of seafood in this
tomato and wine sauce will be wonderful.*

Serves 4

¾ lb. linguine

Cook in boiling water until al dente (firm to the bite). Drain and set aside. Meanwhile, prepare sauce.

⅓ cup olive oil
½ cup clam juice or fish stock
(juice from canned clams is fine)
¼ cup white wine
1 cup tomato sauce

Combine and heat in saucepan for approx. 5 minutes on a medium heat.

4 oz. peeled and deveined shrimp
½ cup canned clams, drained
10 mussels
10 fresh clams (if not available, use more mussels)
4 oz. scallops

Add fresh seafood, cover, and cook just until done and shells open. Do not overcook. Remove mussels and clams. Toss pasta with sauce, place on serving dish, and place mussels and clams around plate to decorate. Serve immediately.

Per serving (¼th)	
Calories:	627
Protein:	34 g
Fat:	22 g
Cholesterol:	99 mg
Carbohydrates:	69 g
Sodium:	402 mg

Spaghetti with Escargots

*Snails are an inexpensive delicacy that
go well with pasta, garlic, and tomatoes.*

Serves 4–6

³/₄ lb. spaghetti	Cook in boiling water until al dente (firm to the bite). Drain and set aside. Meanwhile, prepare sauce.
¹/₄ cup oil	Heat in large skillet.
2 tsp. crushed garlic ***1 small onion, chopped*** ***dash of red pepper*** ***(optional)***	Add and cook until onions are soft.
2 tbsp. chopped parsley ***(1 tsp. dry)*** ***12 oz. crushed tomatoes*** ***(fresh or canned), with*** ***juice***	Add and allow to cook for approx. 10–15 minutes, on a low heat, stirring occasionally.
1 small can of snails, ***drained***	Add to sauce and cook 3 more minutes. Add pasta and toss.
¹/₃ cup Parmesan or ***Romano cheese***	Sprinkle on pasta and serve.

Per serving (¹/₆th)

Calories:	352
Protein:	13 g
Fat:	12 g
Cholesterol:	15 mg
Carbohydrates:	47 g
Sodium:	192 mg

Fettuccine with Shellfish and Mushrooms

Any variety of shellfish makes this pasta a light entrée.

Serves 4–6

1 lb. fettuccine	Cook in boiling water until al dente (firm to the bite). Drain and set aside. Meanwhile, prepare sauce.
2 tbsp. oil	Heat in large saucepan.
1½ lbs. seafood (any combination of shrimp, scallops, or lobster) 1 tbsp. crushed garlic	Add to oil and sauté for 1 minute.
¼ cup white wine ½ cup clam juice *	Add to above, and over a low heat, simmer until seafood is just barely cooked, approx. 3–5 minutes, being careful not to overcook.
10 small mushrooms, sliced ½ tomato, diced	Add and simmer for 1 minute.
½ cup soft butter, cut in pieces	Add slowly until all is incorporated. Add pasta and toss. Serve with Parmesan cheese.
Parmesan cheese chopped parsley for garnish	

*If unable to obtain clam juice, use liquid from canned clams or other fish stock.

Per serving (⅙th)

Calories: 609

Protein: 36 g

Fat: 24 g

Cholesterol: 171 mg

Carbohydrates: 60 g

Sodium: 417 mg

Angel Hair Pasta
with Smoked Salmon

*The combination of smoked salmon
and vodka in a light, creamy wine
sauce is fabulous over thin pasta.*

Serves 4–6

	1 lb. thin pasta (capellini, spaghettini, angel hair)	Cook in boiling water until firm to the bite (al dente). Drain and set aside.
	2 tbsp. butter **½ cup chopped onion** **1½ tsp. chopped garlic**	Heat butter in large skillet. Add onion and garlic and sauté until onion becomes soft.
	5 oz. smoked salmon, cut into strips	Add and sauté until color changes to a pale orange, approx. 1–2 minutes.
	½ cup vodka	Pour in vodka. Flame it carefully or cook approx. 30 seconds on high heat. Remove salmon mixture from pan and set aside. Leave liquid in pan. Place pan back on stove.
	½ cup white wine **¾ cup fish stock (or clam juice)**	Add to pan and bring to a boil for approx. 2 minutes.
	1¼ cups heavy cream	Add and cook over medium heat for approx. 5 minutes. Add salmon mixture and simmer.
	pepper **2 tsp. black caviar (fish roe), optional**	Add to taste. Add pasta to sauce, combine over low heat until well-combined. Serve with (caviar) fish roe if desired.

Per serving (⅙th)

Calories:	538
Protein:	16 g
Fat:	24 g
Cholesterol:	83 mg
Carbohydrates:	60 g
Sodium:	1583 mg

Spinach-and-Ricotta-Filled Cannelloni in a Vegetable Sauce
Donatello, San Francisco

*Crepes (Crespelle) Filled
with Cheese and
Spinach*
Centro, Toronto

Italian Rice with
Spring Vegetables
Primavera, New York

*Fettuccine with Mussels,
Shrimp, and Parsley*
Michela's, Boston

Fettuccine with Calamari and Eggplant

The combination of calamari and eggplant tastes best over black squid pasta.

Serves 4

³/₄ lb. fettuccine (preferably black squid pasta)
Cook in boiling water until al dente (firm to the bite). Drain and set aside. Meanwhile, prepare sauce.

6 tbsp. olive oil
Heat in large skillet.

8 oz. eggplant, cut into cubes
2 tsp. crushed garlic
Sauté until eggplant has a golden color, approx. 5 minutes.

10 oz. calamari (squid), sliced into ¹/₄" rings
8 oz. fish stock (or clam juice)
8 oz. diced tomatoes
dash of chili pepper (fresh or dry) to taste
Add to above and cook on a medium heat for approx. 5 minutes. Add pasta, toss, and serve.

Per serving (¹/₄th)	
Calories:	656
Protein:	31 g
Fat:	27 g
Cholesterol:	59 mg
Carbohydrates:	70 g
Sodium:	219 mg

Linguine with Shrimp and Basil Sauce

Thin pasta coated with shrimp and tomato pieces.

Serves 4

¾ *lb. linguine*	Cook in boiling water until al dente (firm to the bite). Drain and set aside. Meanwhile, prepare sauce.
⅓ *cup olive oil*	Heat in large skillet.
2 *tsp. crushed garlic* *pinch red pepper* 6–10 *basil leaves, chopped* *(1 tsp. dry)*	Add and sauté for 1 minute.
12 *oz. medium shrimp,* *peeled and deveined* 12 *oz. tomatoes, chopped* *(preferably Italian plum)* *salt to taste*	Add and sauté just until shrimp are pink, approx. 3 minutes.
¼ *cup Parmesan cheese*	Add pasta, toss, and serve with Parmesan cheese.

Per serving (¼th)	
Calories:	627
Protein:	34 g
Fat:	23 g
Cholesterol:	131 mg
Carbohydrates:	69 g
Sodium:	275 mg

96

Fettuccine with Mushrooms and Clams

*A delicious standard dish
with a creamy clam sauce.*

Serves 4–6

1 lb. fettuccine	Cook in boiling water until firm to the bite (al dente). Drain and set aside. Meanwhile, prepare sauce.
3 tbsp. olive oil	Heat in skillet.
1 cup chopped mushrooms	Sauté until mushrooms are golden.
1 tsp. chopped garlic **1 tbsp. chopped parsley**	Add and sauté for 2 minutes.
1 (10-oz.) can of clams	Save only half the liquid and add clams and reserved juice to above.
$1/3$ cup dry white wine	Add and cook on medium heat approx. 5 minutes.
$1^1/2$ cups heavy cream **salt and pepper**	Add to above and simmer approx. 5 minutes. Season with salt and pepper.
1 tbsp. butter **$3/4$ cup Parmesan cheese** **parsley for garnish**	Add to above. Mix well and serve over pasta. Sprinkle with more Parmesan and parsley as a garnish.

Per serving (¼th)

Calories:	594
Protein:	16 g
Fat:	31 g
Cholesterol:	103 mg
Carbohydrates:	60 g
Sodium:	87 mg

Fusilli with Shrimps and Crabmeat

Herbs with seafood in
a garlic oil sauce.

Serves 2–4

½ lb. fusilli (pasta twists)	Cook in boiling water until firm to the bite (al dente). Drain and set aside.
3 tbsp. olive oil *1 tsp. chopped garlic*	Heat in large pan until garlic becomes brown.
6 oz. shrimp, *shelled and deveined*	Add and sauté until just barely cooked.
3 tbsp. white wine *8 oz. chopped tomatoes* *(preferably Italian plum)* *6 leaves chopped basil* *(1 tsp. dry)* *12 leaves chopped oregano* *(1 tsp. dry)* *1 tbsp. chopped parsley* *(1 tsp. dry)*	Add to above and simmer for 5 minutes.
2 oz. crabmeat	Add to above, add pasta, and toss until blended.
basil for garnish	Garnish with fresh basil leaves.

Per serving (¼th)

Calories:	380
Protein:	20 g
Fat:	12 g
Cholesterol:	78 mg
Carbohydrates:	46 g
Sodium:	96 mg

Fettuccine with Smoked Salmon and Fresh Dill

A creamy dill sauce coats the smoked salmon and pasta.

Serves 2–4

½ lb. fettuccine	Cook in boiling water until al dente (firm to the bite). Drain and set aside.
1 tbsp. butter	Heat in large pan.
1 tbsp. chopped shallots (or white bulb of green onion)	Cook onions until soft.
2 tbsp. chopped dill (1½ tsp. dry) *4 oz. smoked salmon (finely sliced—julienned)* *⅓ cup dry vermouth*	Add and cook on a high heat for 1 minute.
¾ cup heavy cream *pepper to taste (preferably white)*	Add and cook on high for approx. 2 minutes or until cream thickens slightly.
	Add noodles and toss mixture in pan until well-mixed.
dill sprigs for garnish *salmon caviar for garnish*	Garnish with dill sprigs and 1 tsp. salmon caviar if desired.

Per serving (¼th)

Calories:	434
Protein:	14 g
Fat:	21 g
Cholesterol:	75 mg
Carbohydrates:	45 g
Sodium:	1754 mg

Fettuccine with Scallops in Tomato Sauce

This dish with plum tomatoes, scallops, and red onions is best served over black squid pasta if possible. If not, white pasta will do.

Serves 4

¾ lb. fettuccine (preferably black squid pasta)	Cook in boiling water until al dente (firm to the bite). Drain and set aside. Meanwhile, prepare sauce.
3 tbsp. olive oil	Heat in large skillet.
1 tsp. crushed garlic **½ medium red onion, sliced**	Add and cook until onion is soft.
3 lb. tomatoes (preferably Italian plum)	Purée and add to above. Cook on a medium heat for 15–20 minutes, stirring occasionally.
18 leaves chopped fresh basil (1 tbsp. dry) **salt and pepper to taste**	Add, stir, and remove from heat. Set aside.
12 medium scallops, sliced **1 tsp. butter**	In a small pan, sauté briefly just until seared on both sides. Add to above sauce and toss with pasta. Serve immediately.

Per serving (¼th)

Calories:	551
Protein:	26 g
Fat:	13 g
Cholesterol:	30 mg
Carbohydrates:	83 g
Sodium:	235 mg

Angel Hair Pasta with Wild Mushrooms and Shrimp

Paper thin pasta coated with a variety of mushrooms, shrimps, and tomatoes.

Serves 4

½ lb. angel hair (or any fine strands—capellini, spaghettini, etc.)	Cook in boiling water until al dente (firm to the bite). Drain and set aside. Meanwhile, prepare sauce.
2 tbsp. olive oil	Heat in large skillet.
4 oz. sliced mushrooms (preferably wild such as chanterelle, shiitake, or oyster) *1 tsp. chopped garlic* *6 oz. shrimp, peeled and deveined*	Add and sauté just until shrimp turns pink.
2 tbsp. white wine	Add and stir.
8 oz. chopped tomatoes (preferably Italian plum) *pinch of parsley, thyme, hot pepper, salt* *1 tbsp. chopped basil (1 tsp. dry)* *3 tbsp. Parmesan cheese (optional)*	Add and stir just until combined.
black pepper and parsley for garnish	Add pasta and garnish with parsley and pepper.

Per serving (¼th)

Calories:	313
Protein:	13 g
Fat:	7 g
Cholesterol:	31 mg
Carbohydrates:	46 g
Sodium:	93 mg

Pasta with Tuna in an Herb Tomato Sauce

The combination of a mildly spicy tomato sauce with tuna served over twisted pasta is ideal for a light meal.

Serves 4–6

Per serving (¹⁄₆th)
Calories: 463
Protein: 23 g
Fat: 13 g
Cholesterol: 33 mg
Carbohydrates: 63 g
Sodium: 603 mg

1 lb. fusilli (spiral or twisted pasta)
Cook in boiling water until firm to the bite (al dente). Drain and set aside.

2 tbsp. olive oil
Heat in large skillet.

2 crushed garlic cloves
Add and sauté for 1 minute.

4–6 anchovy fillets
Add and cook until anchovies become pastelike.

2 tbsp. red wine
1 (7-oz.) can tuna, drained
1 (28-oz.) can tomatoes, (preferably Italian plum), with juice
Add to above, stirring occasionally, until tomatoes are broken up. Cook over a medium heat for approx. 20 minutes.

pinch crushed red pepper flakes
¹⁄₂ tsp. dried oregano
¹⁄₄ tsp. dried thyme
¹⁄₂ tsp. dried basil, or 6 fresh leaves, chopped
1 tbsp. fresh parsley, chopped
freshly ground pepper
1 tbsp. butter
Add to above and add cooked pasta. Mix well. Pour into serving dish.

¹⁄₂ cup Parmesan cheese
Add to above and serve immediately.

102

Fettuccine with Smoked Salmon and Vodka

Smoked salmon in a creamy vodka sauce is heavenly over this pasta.

Serves 4–6

¾ lb. fettuccine	Cook in boiling water until al dente (firm to the bite). Drain and set aside. Meanwhile, prepare sauce.
2 tbsp. olive oil **2 tbsp. butter**	Heat in large skillet.
1 garlic clove, crushed **1 tbsp. finely chopped onion**	Add and sauté for 2 minutes.
4 medium tomatoes, diced	Add and cook on medium heat for 5 minutes. Lower heat.
8 oz. smoked salmon, chopped **4 tbsp. vodka** **1 cup heavy cream**	Add, cover, and simmer for 10 more minutes, stirring occasionally.
pepper to taste	Add along with pasta and toss well.
¼ cup Parmesan cheese **1 oz. caviar (fish roe), optional**	Serve with pasta.

(If a saltier taste is desired, add smoked salmon at the same time as tomatoes.)

Per serving (⅙th)	
Calories:	520
Protein:	18 g
Fat:	29 g
Cholesterol:	84 mg
Carbohydrates:	49 g
Sodium:	2485 mg

Linguine with Mussels, Sun-Dried Tomatoes, and Olives

A pasta coated with red peppers, garlic, tomatoes, and fresh mussels in a light saffron sauce.

Serves 4

³/₄ lb. linguine	Cook in boiling water just until firm to the bite (al dente). Drain and set aside.
1 tbsp. oil *¹/₂ chopped small onion* *¹/₂ cup white wine* *1 lb. mussels*	In covered saucepan, cook approx. 5 minutes or until mussels open. Remove mussels from shells and reserve.
2 tbsp. olive oil	Heat in large skillet.
1 small onion, diced *2 crushed garlic cloves* *1 medium red pepper, sliced* *4 small tomatoes, diced*	Add and sauté until vegetables become soft.
salt and pepper to taste *¹/₄ cup green sliced olives* *¹/₃ cup chopped sun-dried tomatoes* *¹/₄ cup fresh basil (1¹/₂ tsp. dry)*	Add to above along with reserved mussels. Add pasta, toss, and serve.

Per serving (¹/₄th)	
Calories:	519
Protein:	18 g
Fat:	15 g
Cholesterol:	33 mg
Carbohydrates:	76 g
Sodium:	654 mg

Fettuccine with Mussels, Shrimps, and Parsley

Fresh mussels steamed in a white wine garlic sauce is delicious with this unusual pasta dish.

Serves 4–6

³/₄ lb. fettuccine	Cook in boiling water until al dente (firm to the bite). Drain and set aside. Meanwhile, prepare sauce.
2¹/₂ slices stale bread *¹/₃ cup red wine vinegar*	Soak for 5 minutes. Squeeze out excess.
³/₄ bunch parsley leaves *¹/₂ tbsp. capers* *4 anchovy fillets* *2 garlic cloves, crushed*	Place in blender along with above bread. Purée.
5 tbsp. olive oil	Add to above to make a smooth paste. Set aside.
approx. 20 mussels *¹/₂ cup white wine* *2 crushed garlic cloves*	Steam mussels with wine and garlic just until open, approx. 5 minutes. Remove from shell and keep mussels in liquid. Set aside.
3 oz. chopped bacon (preferably Italian pancetta)	Sauté for 2 minutes in large saucepan. (Either pour off fat or keep.)
12 oz. medium shrimp, peeled and deveined	Add and sauté just until pink. Add mussels and their liquid and heat for 1 minute. Add above parsley sauce. Add pasta and toss well.

Per serving (¹/₆th)	
Calories:	576
Protein:	35 g
Fat:	22 g
Cholesterol:	123 mg
Carbohydrates:	53 g
Sodium:	310 mg

Spaghettini with Shellfish

Any shellfish would be fine with this olive and garlic sauce, but lobster is at the top of the list.

Serves 4–6

¾ lb. spaghettini or thin pasta

Cook in boiling water until al dente (firm to the bite). Drain and set aside. Meanwhile, prepare sauce.

1½ lbs. cooked shellfish (shrimp, scallops, lobster, or any combination)

Cut into chunks.

¾ bunch chopped parsley leaves (2 tbsp. dry)
½ cup olive oil
2 cloves crushed garlic
½ small lemon, squeezed
salt and pepper to taste

Combine in large bowl, add shellfish and pasta, and toss well.

Per serving (⅙th)	
Calories:	507
Protein:	34 g
Fat:	20 g
Cholesterol:	135 mg
Carbohydrates:	45 g
Sodium:	250 mg

Tagliatelle with Shrimp, Garlic, and Parmesan Cheese

Delicate shrimp in a garlic wine sauce.

Serves 2–4

½ lb. pasta (fettuccine or tagliatelle)	Cook in boiling water until al dente (firm to the bite). Drain and set aside. Meanwhile, prepare sauce.
2 tbsp. olive oil	Heat in large skillet.
8 oz. shrimp, peeled and deveined *1 tbsp. crushed garlic*	Add and sauté until shrimps are just cooked, approx. 3–4 minutes. Remove from heat.
¼ cup white wine *salt and pepper*	Add and stir.
1 tbsp. oil *1½ tbsp. butter*	Add until well-blended. Add pasta and toss.
3 tbsp. Parmesan cheese	Sprinkle over pasta and serve.

Per serving (¼th)	
Calories:	430
Protein:	22 g
Fat:	17 g
Cholesterol:	98 mg
Carbohydrates:	44 g
Sodium:	249 mg

Fettuccine with Scallops and Mushrooms

A variety of mushrooms with tender scallops in a creamy sauce.

Serves 4–6

¾ lb. fettuccine	Cook in boiling water until al dente (firm to the bite). Drain and set aside. Meanwhile, prepare sauce.
2 tbsp. butter **2 tbsp. oil**	Heat in large skillet.
3 cups chopped mushrooms (preferably wild mushrooms)	Add and cook until soft.
1 lb. scallops	Add and sauté until just under-cooked. (Do not overcook.)
1¼ cups heavy cream	Add and cook on a moderate heat for approx. 3–4 minutes, being careful not to overcook the scallops.
2 tbsp. chopped basil (1 tsp. dry)	Add to above along with pasta and toss.

Per serving (⅙th)
Calories: 542
Protein: 25 g
Fat: 28 g
Cholesterol: 112 mg
Carbohydrates: 49 g
Sodium: 246 mg

Fettuccine with Calamari in a Spicy Mediterranean Sauce

Squid in a garlic and tomato sauce with black olives.

Serves 4–5

¾ lb. fettuccine or tagliatelle	Cook in boiling water until al dente (firm to the bite). Drain and set aside. Meanwhile, prepare sauce.
¼ cup olive oil	Heat in large saucepan.
3 crushed garlic cloves	Add and cook until golden.
2 tbsp. tiny capers (or to taste) **4 anchovy fillets, mashed** **approx. 20 black olives, pitted and chopped**	Add and cook 1 minute.
1 (28-oz.) can tomatoes, with juice (preferably Italian plum)	Add and stir until combined. Simmer for approx. 15–20 minutes, or until sauce has thickened. Stir often to break up tomatoes.
red pepper flakes to taste **1 tbsp. oregano (dry)** **1 tbsp. basil (dry)** **1 lb. cleaned calamari, cut into thin rings**	Add to saucepan and stir for approx. 3 minutes, just until calamari is cooked, but not tough. Add pasta and toss well.
¼ cup Parmesan cheese **fresh chopped parsley**	Add to pasta and serve.

Per serving (⅕th)

Calories:	617
Protein:	39 g
Fat:	24 g
Cholesterol:	85 mg
Carbohydrates:	59 g
Sodium:	1183 mg

Linguine with Curried Seafood

The amount of curry can vary according to taste. This is definitely one of the best pasta dishes I have ever tasted. A lot of ingredients, but well worth the time.

Serves 4–6

1 lb. linguine or tagliatelle	Cook in boiling water until al dente (firm to the bite). Drain and set aside. Meanwhile, prepare sauce.
¼ cup butter	Heat in skillet.
1½ cups chopped onions **½ cup chopped carrots** **½ cup chopped celery** **1 tbsp. crushed garlic**	Add and cook until soft, approx. 10 minutes.
1½ cups diced unpeeled green apple (approx. 1 apple) **¾ cup chopped tomato** **½ tsp. dry thyme** **1 bay leaf**	Add and cook on a medium heat for 5 minutes.
2 tbsp. curry powder * (or to taste) **¼ cup flour**	Add and cook on a low heat 3 more minutes.
2 cups chicken stock (hot)	Add, reduce heat, and simmer, uncovered, about 15 minutes.

*The chef recommends as much as ¼ cup curry, but use according to your taste.

(continued)

Per serving (⅙th)

Calories:	663
Protein:	28 g
Fat:	28 g
Cholesterol:	139 mg
Carbohydrates:	75 g
Sodium:	685 mg

110

Linguine with Curried Seafood *(continued)*

¹⁄₄ cup heavy cream	Add and simmer 3 minutes. Strain sauce, pressing vegetables with the back of a spoon to squeeze out liquid. (Set strained sauce aside. Toss out vegetables.)
¹⁄₃ cup butter	Melt in large skillet.
8 oz. chopped mushrooms	Add and sauté for 3 minutes.
8 oz. medium shrimp, peeled, deveined, and cut in half	Add and sauté until seafood is barely cooked.
8 oz. scallops (preferably bay)	Add pasta and curry sauce to seafood mixture and toss thoroughly. Serve immediately.

Capellini with Seafood

Fine pasta surrounded by a variety of seafood in a tomato garlic sauce.

Serves 4–6 people

³⁄₄ lb. thin pasta (capellini, angel hair, etc.)

Cook in boiling water just until al dente (firm to the bite). Drain and set aside. Meanwhile, prepare sauce.

4 tbsp. olive oil
2 tsp. garlic cloves, crushed
dash of red pepper to taste
¹⁄₂ lb. diced tomatoes (preferably Italian plum)

Cook in a large skillet on a medium heat for approx. 5 minutes, just until tomatoes are soft.

6 oz. shrimp, peeled and deveined
6 oz. small scallops (preferably bay)
approx. 10 mussels
approx. 15 clams (if unable to obtain, use more mussels)

Add and cook just until seafood is cooked and shells open, approx. 5 minutes, stirring constantly.

¹⁄₂ cup clam juice or fish stock
¹⁄₂ cup consommé (chicken)
2 tbsp. chopped parsley

Add to above and bring to a boil. Add cooked pasta, toss, and serve.

Per serving (¹⁄₆th)

Calories:	438
Protein:	31 g
Fat:	12 g
Cholesterol:	86 mg
Carbohydrates:	48 g
Sodium:	277 mg

Linguine with Shrimp and Sun-Dried Tomatoes

Shrimp and sun-dried tomatoes in a light, creamy cheese sauce.

Serves 4–6

¾ lb. linguine or fettuccine	Cook in boiling water until firm to the bite (al dente). Drain and set aside. Meanwhile, prepare sauce.
8 asparagus spears, cut into 1" pieces	Boil for 2 minutes. Drain and set aside.
4 tbsp. butter	Heat in large skillet.
½ cup chopped onions 2 tbsp. chopped shallots or onions	Add and sauté until onions are golden.
10 oz. shrimps, peeled and deveined, cut into small pieces 6 sun-dried tomatoes, chopped	Add to onion mixture with cooked asparagus and cook just until shrimp turns pink.
1 cup heavy cream	Add and cook on a medium heat approx. 2 minutes, until sauce thickens.
¼ cup Parmesan cheese	Add to sauce and add fettuccine. Stir well and serve.

Per serving (⅙th)

Calories:	494
Protein:	20 g
Fat:	24 g
Cholesterol:	139 mg
Carbohydrates:	47 g
Sodium:	220 mg

Capellini with Asparagus and Scallops

*Small, sweet scallops in
a garlic tomato sauce.*

Serves 4–6

³/₄ lb. thin pasta (capellini, spaghettini, angel hair) — Cook in boiling water until al dente (firm to the bite). Drain and set aside. Meanwhile, prepare sauce.

2 tbsp. olive oil — Heat in large skillet.

2–3 crushed garlic cloves
2 green onions or scallions, sliced thin
8 oz. asparagus, cut into small pieces
6 large basil leaves, chopped (1 tsp. dry)
5–6 small tomatoes, diced (preferably Italian plum)
salt and pepper
— Add and sauté for 5 minutes.

¹/₂ cup water — Add and simmer until the tomatoes have blended well, approx. 4 minutes.

1 lb. scallops (preferably bay) — Add and cook just until slightly underdone. Do not overcook scallops. Add pasta and toss.

¹/₄ cup Parmesan (optional) — If desired, add cheese and serve.

Per serving (¹/₆th)	
Calories:	338
Protein:	22 g
Fat:	6 g
Cholesterol:	32 mg
Carbohydrates:	46 g
Sodium:	251 mg

114

Angel Hair Pasta with Tomato and Seafood

A light pasta with morsels of seafood and tomatoes.

Serves 6

Ingredients	Instructions
¾ lb. angel hair pasta or spaghetti	Cook in boiling water until al dente (firm to the bite). Drain.
10 leaves basil (2 tsp. dry) small bunch rosemary chopped (1 tsp. dry) small bunch sage chopped (½ tsp. dry) small bunch oregano chopped (1 tsp. dry) 4 crushed garlic cloves ½ cup white wine ½ cup olive oil	Combine in covered saucepan and cook for 10 minutes on a low heat. Strain and save liquid.
1½ lbs. diced tomatoes (preferably Italian plum)	Add to above liquid and simmer approx. 20–25 minutes, until the consistency of tomato sauce.
1 lb. combination of cooked mixed seafood (shrimp, scallops, mussels, clams, etc.)	Cut into small pieces. Add to above sauce and mix. Add pasta, toss, and serve.

Per serving (⅙th)	
Calories:	473
Protein:	22 g
Fat:	20 g
Cholesterol:	58 mg
Carbohydrates:	50 g
Sodium:	124 mg

Linguine with Baby Clams in Tomato Sauce

Baby clams with crushed tomatoes are subtle in this pasta dish.

Serves 4

¾ lb. linguine

Cook in boiling water until firm to the bite (al dente). Drain. Set aside. Meanwhile, prepare sauce.

⅓ cup oil
1 onion, chopped

In large skillet, cook onions in oil until soft.

16 oz. crushed tomatoes, with juice
(preferably Italian plum)
8 basil leaves (1½ tsp. dry)
1 tbsp. chopped parsley

Add and cook on a low heat for approx. 15 minutes, until thickened.

5 oz. baby clams
Parmesan cheese to taste

Add to above and cook 5 more minutes. Add cooked pasta to sauce, mix well, and serve with Parmesan cheese.

Per serving (¼th)
Calories: 571
Protein: 17 g
Fat: 23 g
Cholesterol: 20 mg
Carbohydrates: 72 g
Sodium: 240 mg

Fettuccine with Shrimp and Radicchio Vinaigrette

A tangy sauce over a bed of pasta interspersed with delicate pieces of shrimp.

Serves 6–8 as an appetizer

Vinaigrette

¹/₃ cup balsamic vinegar *
³/₄ cup plus 2 tbsp. olive oil
2 tbsp. finely chopped shallots or onions
2 tbsp. minced garlic
4 tbsp. chopped fresh basil (1 tsp. dry)
juice of 1 small lemon

Combine in bowl.

1 small head radicchio

Without removing the core, cut into quarters. Place in marinade for at least 2 hours.

12 oz. shrimp, peeled and deveined
1 tbsp. butter

Sauté just until pink. Do not overcook. Set aside. Squeeze excess vinaigrette from radicchio, and reserve it for later. Remove core. Cook the radicchio over a medium heat until soft, approx. 5 minutes. Purée radicchio with reserved vinaigrette until smooth. Set aside.

1 lb. fettuccine

Cook in boiling water until firm to the bite (al dente). Drain and combine with radicchio sauce and cooked shrimps. Serve.

*Balsamic vinegar can be bought at most supermarkets or food specialty shops.

Per serving (⅛th)	
Calories:	466
Protein:	18 g
Fat:	24 g
Cholesterol:	67 mg
Carbohydrates:	45 g
Sodium:	80 mg

Baked or Stuffed Pasta

Pasta Shells Stuffed with Cheese in a Creamy Tomato Sauce

This mild cheese filling would be suitable for any homemade stuffed pasta such as ravioli or tortellini.

Preheat oven to 375°F
Baking pan
Serves 4–5

½ lb. jumbo pasta shells or 12 manicotti shells	Cook in boiling water until al dente (firm to the bite). Drain and set aside. Meanwhile, prepare sauce.
1 cup ricotta cheese *½ cup Parmesan cheese* *¼ cup soft mild cheese, grated (such as fontina, Havarti, brick, etc.)* *4 tbsp. finely chopped chives or green onions* *2 egg yolks*	Mix in a bowl until combined. Stuff pasta shells.
1 tbsp. butter	Butter the bottom of the baking dish.
¼ cup heavy cream	Pour in dish. Place pasta in dish.
2 cups prepared tomato sauce	Pour over shells.
⅓ cup Parmesan cheese	Sprinkle over shells. Cover and bake until hot, approx. 20 minutes.
chives for garnish	Garnish with chopped chives.

Per serving (⅕th)	
Calories:	492
Protein:	24 g
Fat:	24 g
Cholesterol:	180 mg
Carbohydrates:	40 g
Sodium:	612 mg

Artichoke-Filled Pasta with Tomato Sauce*

Artichokes combined with a variety of cheeses are delicious with this tomato garlic sauce.

Preheat oven to 350°F
Serves 4–6

12 cannelloni or manicotti shells	Cook in boiling water until al dente (firm to the bite). Drain and set aside. Meanwhile, prepare sauce.
8 oz. artichoke hearts	Use either canned or cook yourself (see page 15). Cut hearts into thin slices.
2 tbsp. olive oil	Heat in skillet.
½ small onion, diced **1 large garlic clove, crushed**	Add and cook until onion is soft.
3 tbsp. white wine	Add along with artichokes and cook until liquid has evaporated, approx. 3 minutes. Process in food processor just until chopped. (Do not purée.)
4 oz. ricotta cheese **2 oz. blue cheese (Gorgonzola)** **1 egg yolk** **1 tsp. chopped parsley** **salt and pepper**	Add to above and process briefly. Do not overblend. Fill shells with approx. 1 tbsp. artichoke filling and place in baking pan. Prepare sauce.

Per serving (⅙th)

Calories:	303
Protein:	10 g
Fat:	15 g
Cholesterol:	58 mg
Carbohydrates:	32 g
Sodium:	469 mg

*If desired, prepare stuffed pasta such as tortellini, ravioli, etc. using this filling. See page 10.

(continued)

**Artichoke-Filled Pasta
with Tomato Sauce** *(continued)*

Sauce

2 tbsp. olive oil	Heat in skillet.
½ carrot, finely chopped *1 garlic clove, crushed*	Add and cook for 1 minute.
16 oz. unripened tomatoes, * * *coarsely chopped* *1 cup chicken broth* *1 bay leaf* *¼ cup chopped basil* *(1 tbsp. dry)* *salt and pepper to taste*	Add and simmer until thick, stirring occasionally, about 15 minutes. Remove bay leaf, pour over cannelloni, cover, and bake approx. 20–25 minutes, until hot.

**The greener the tomatoes, the better the sauce.

Salmon-Filled Shells with Tomato Vodka Sauce*

A light salmon filling with a sauce of diced tomatoes and cream.

Preheat oven to 350°F
Serves 4–6

2 tbsp. olive oil	Heat in skillet.
1 tbsp. minced green onion (white part)	Add and stir for 1 minute.
¾ lb. skinned, boned salmon, cut into small cubes **3 tbsp. white wine** **1 tbsp. minced fresh parsley (1 tsp. dry)** **½ tsp. minced fresh thyme (¼ tsp. dry)**	Add and cook until salmon is cooked outside, but pink inside, about 3–5 minutes. Purée in food processor.
2 tbsp. Parmesan cheese **1 egg yolk** **3 tbsp. butter** **salt, pepper, and a dash of hot pepper**	Add and purée just until mixed. Cool before filling. Meanwhile, cook pasta.
12–16 jumbo pasta shells	Cook in boiling water until al dente (firm to the bite). Drain and set aside. Meanwhile, prepare sauce.

Per serving (⅙th)
Calories: 518
Protein: 22 g
Fat: 34 g
Cholesterol: 151 mg
Carbohydrates: 28 g
Sodium: 291 mg

*As an alternative, prepare stuffed pasta such as ravioli, tortellini, etc. using this filling. See page 10.

(continued)

**Salmon-Filled Shells with
Tomato Vodka Sauce** *(continued)*

Sauce

2 tbsp. butter	Melt in skillet.
2 green onions, chopped	Add and cook for 1 minute.
1/3 cup vodka	Add and boil approx. 1 minute.
12 oz. chopped tomatoes *1 cup heavy cream* *1 tsp. crushed peppercorns* *(pink if possible)* *salt to taste*	Add and simmer until thickened, approx. 5–8 minutes. Fill shells with salmon filling. Lay in baking pan and pour sauce over. Cover and bake until hot, approx. 25 minutes.

Lasagna with Bell Peppers, Eggplant, and Zucchini

An unusual lasagna with a delicious variety of vegetables.

Preheat oven to broil
9″ × 13″ baking pan
Serves 8

Approx. 9–10 lasagna sheets (13″ × 3″ each)	Cook in boiling water until al dente (firm to the bite). Drain and set aside. Meanwhile, prepare sauce.
3 cups prepared tomato sauce	Set aside.
2 roasted red or yellow peppers	Broil for approx. 10 minutes or until charred, turning constantly. Lower temperature to 350°F. Rinse in cold water, remove top, peel, and de-seed. Slice in thin strips. Set aside.
1 small eggplant ***1 medium zucchini*** ***⅓ cup olive oil***	Slice vegetables thin, cut pieces in half, and dust with flour. Sauté vegetables (keep separated) in oil until barely cooked. Set aside.
2 tbsp. olive oil ***8 oz. mushrooms, sliced*** ***¼ small onion, diced***	Sauté until vegetables are soft. Set aside.

(continued)

Per serving (⅛th)

Calories:	439
Protein:	19 g
Fat:	22 g
Cholesterol:	28 mg
Carbohydrates:	41 g
Sodium:	413 mg

**Lasagna with Bell Peppers,
Eggplant, and Zucchini** *(continued)*

12 oz. mozzarella, sliced	Set aside.
½ cup Parmesan	Set aside.

Assembly

Pour approx. ¾ cup tomato sauce in pan. Place 3 lasagna sheets down. Place eggplant and half of peppers over top, half of mozzarella, half of Parmesan, and 1 cup of tomato sauce. Place 3 more lasagna sheets over top, follow with zucchini and mushroom mixture, remaining peppers, remaining mozzarella cheese, and top with last lasagna sheets, tomato sauce, and Parmesan cheese. Cover and bake for approx. 45 minutes, until hot.

Spinach-and-Ricotta-Filled Cannelloni in a Vegetable Sauce*

This rich vegetable sauce over this creamy cheese filling is wonderful.

Preheat oven to 350°F
Serves 4–6

12 cannelloni or manicotti shells

Cook in boiling water with a little oil just until al dente (firm to the bite). Drain, rinse, and set aside. Meanwhile, prepare filling.

Filling

Half a 10-oz. frozen spinach package, thawed
$1/2$ cup water

Cook in a covered pan for approx. 5 minutes. Drain and squeeze out excess liquid. Chop fine.

$1 1/4$ cups ricotta cheese
$3/4$ cup Parmesan cheese
1 egg yolk
$1/4$ tsp. nutmeg

Combine and add to spinach. Mix well. Place approx. 1 tbsp. into pasta shells. Place side by side in baking dish. Cover until sauce is prepared.

Sauce

Per serving (⅙th)	
Calories:	418
Protein:	17 g
Fat:	25 g
Cholesterol:	115 mg
Carbohydrates:	30 g
Sodium:	482 mg

1 medium carrot, finely diced
2 small zucchini, finely diced (or one zucchini and one yellow summer squash)

Place in boiling water for 1 minute. Drain.

*To simplify, ready-made stuffed pasta such as ravioli, tortellini, etc. can be used instead of manicotti, with a cheese and/or spinach filling.

(continued)

**Spinach-and-Ricotta-Filled Cannelloni
in a Vegetable Sauce** *(continued)*

¹/₄ cup butter *2 tbsp. chopped basil* *(1 tsp. dry)*	Sauté diced vegetables in butter and basil for 2–3 minutes.
1¹/₂ cups water	Add to vegetables and bring to a vigorous boil until the water has reduced to half, approx. 5 minutes.
¹/₄ cup butter	Add butter and continue reducing until slightly thickened, approx. 2 minutes. Remove from heat.
3 tbsp. Parmesan cheese	Add to above and stir. Pour over cannelloni, cover, and bake approx. 20–30 minutes, until hot.

Scallop-and-Mushroom-Stuffed Shells*

*The combination of mushrooms, tomatoes,
and bite-size pieces of scallops are
outstanding in any filled pasta.*

Preheat oven to 350°F
1 large baking dish
Serves 4–6

16–20 jumbo pasta shells	Cook in boiling water until al dente (firm to the bite). Drain, rinse, and set aside.
1 medium tomato, diced	Set aside.
1 tbsp. olive oil ***8 oz. scallops***	Heat in skillet. Sauté scallops in oil briefly. Drain and set aside to cool. Dice.
8 oz. mushrooms (preferably wild such as oyster or shiitake)	Chop coarsely. Set aside.
1 tbsp. olive oil ***1 small onion, diced***	Heat in skillet. Sauté in oil until onion is soft.
1 sprig thyme (¹⁄₄ tsp. dry)	Add along with mushrooms and cook until mushrooms are soft. Drain and set aside to cool. Add diced tomato and diced scallops and combine. Fill pasta shells and place in baking dish.

Per serving (¹⁄₆th)
Calories: 249
Protein: 13 g
Fat: 8 g
Cholesterol: 24 mg
Carbohydrates: 29 g
Sodium: 278 mg

*If desired, homemade stuffed pasta such as ravioli, tortellini, etc. can be used for this filling. See page 10.

(continued)

130

Scallop-and-Mushroom-Stuffed Shells *(continued)*

Sauce

3 tbsp. chopped shallots or onions
1 tsp. olive oil
sprig of thyme (dash of dry)
6 whole peppercorns
pinch of saffron

Combine ingredients and cook for 2 minutes.

½ cup white wine
⅛ cup brandy

Add, turn up heat, and boil until liquid is reduced by half, approx. 3 minutes.

1 cup chicken or fish stock

Add and simmer over moderate heat for about 5 minutes.

½ tbsp. flour
1 tbsp. soft butter

Mix until a smooth paste forms. Add to above sauce and cook for 1 minute, until sauce has thickened. Strain sauce. Pour over cannelloni, cover, and bake for approx. 20 minutes or until hot.

Tortellini with Cheesy Tomato Sauce

Creamy tomato sauce is wonderful over a meat-stuffed pasta.

Preheat oven to 500°F
Serves 4

1 lb. meat-stuffed pasta (tortellini, ravioli, or agnolotti)

Cook in boiling water until al dente (firm to the bite). Drain and set aside. Meanwhile, prepare sauce.

1 cup heavy cream
½ cup prepared tomato sauce
¼ cup Parmesan cheese
1 tbsp. chopped parsley
salt and pepper to taste

In a large skillet, combine and cook on a low heat until the sauce is creamy, approx. 3–5 minutes. Add tortellini and sauté for 3 minutes. Place in baking dish.

2 tbsp. Parmesan cheese

Sprinkle with cheese. Bake for 2–4 minutes, just until cheese begins to brown. Serve immediately.

Per serving (¼th)
Calories: 412
Protein: 16 g
Fat: 29 g
Cholesterol: 199 mg
Carbohydrates: 19 g
Sodium: 277 mg

Mushrooms and Cheese in Pasta Shells

*Puréed mushrooms and tangy cheese are delicious
with this sweet wine sauce. This stuffing is
also ideal with homemade ravioli or tortellini.*

Preheat oven to 350°F
Serves 4–6 as an appetizer

	¹⁄₂ lb. jumbo pasta shells	Cook in boiling water until al dente (firm to the bite). Drain and set aside.
	4 tbsp. olive oil *2 tbsp. crushed garlic* *1 lb. chopped mushrooms* *(common or wild)* *¹⁄₄ cup chopped scallions or green onions*	Heat oil in large skillet. Add garlic and mushrooms and cook on a medium heat until soft. Add scallions to above and cook for 2 minutes.
	1 cup Parmesan or Romano cheese* *(or combined)*	Add and purée mixture in food processor. Fill shells and place in baking dish. Meanwhile, prepare sauce.
	¹⁄₂ cup marsala wine (sweet red wine) *1 tbsp. chopped shallots or green onions*	Heat and cook on a medium heat for approx. 2 minutes.
	¹⁄₂ cup heavy cream	Add and cook for 2 more minutes.
	¹⁄₃ cup soft butter	Add to above until blended.
	¹⁄₂ cup chopped tomatoes *¹⁄₄ cup green peas* *¹⁄₄ cup sliced mushrooms* *(preferably wild)* *salt and pepper to taste*	Add to above and pour over shells. Cover and bake until hot, approx. 30 minutes.

Per serving (¹⁄₆th)

Calories:	462
Protein:	13 g
Fat:	30 g
Cholesterol:	60 mg
Carbohydrates:	36 g
Sodium:	476 mg

*Romano cheese is very sharp tasting.

Salmon Cannelloni with Creamy White Sauce

This light salmon filling would be perfect
for any homemade stuffed pasta.

Preheat oven to 350°F
Serves 4–5

8–10 cannelloni or manicotti shells	Cook in boiling water until al dente (firm to the bite). Drain and set aside.
4 tbsp. butter *1/3 cup chopped shallots or onions* *1/2 tbsp. capers or to taste*	Heat in skillet. Add and cook for 1 minute.
1/2 lb. salmon fillet, cubed	Add and cook until salmon is just slightly cooked.
1 1/2 tbsp. brandy (cognac) *1 bunch chopped dill* *(1 tbsp. dry)*	Add and cook 2 more minutes. Remove and purée in food processor.
1/2 cup heavy cream	Add and blend. Place approx. 1 tbsp. in shells and place in baking dish. Meanwhile, prepare sauce.
1 1/2 tbsp. white wine *1 1/2 tbsp. white wine vinegar* *1 tbsp. chopped shallots or onions*	In saucepan, cook on a medium heat for 1 minute.
1 tsp. crushed garlic *1/3 cup heavy cream* *1/3 cup soft butter* *juice of 1/4 small lemon*	Add garlic and cream and cook for 1 more minute. Add butter until combined, then add juice and mix.
salt and pepper to taste *1 tbsp. chopped dill* *(1/3 tsp. dry)*	Add, mix, and pour over shells. Cover and bake until hot, approx. 25 minutes.

Per serving (1/5th)	
Calories:	488
Protein:	16 g
Fat:	38 g
Cholesterol:	128 mg
Carbohydrates:	20 g
Sodium:	406 mg

Cannelloni with Cheese and Meat Filling

A rich and delicious filling.

Preheat oven to 350°F
Serves 4

10 cannelloni or manicotti shells	Cook in boiling water until firm to the bite (al dente). Rinse in cold water and set aside. Meanwhile, prepare filling.
2 tbsp. olive oil	Heat in skillet.
3 oz. ground beef **3 oz. ground veal**	Add and cook the meat until it is browned, stirring occasionally.
2 tbsp. finely chopped onion **1 tsp. chopped garlic** **1 tbsp. finely chopped carrot** **1 tbsp. finely chopped celery**	Add and cook until vegetables are soft.
1 tbsp. tomato paste **¼ cup red wine**	Add and bring mixture to a boil and cook for approx. 2 minutes. Let mixture cool slightly.
2 oz. grated mozzarella **2 tbsp. ricotta cheese** **2 tbsp. Parmesan cheese** **1 egg** **pinch of nutmeg, rosemary, sage, salt, pepper**	Add to meat mixture and stir well. Place approx. 1 tbsp. of filling into pasta shells. Place in baking dish.
1½ cups prepared tomato sauce	Pour over cannelloni and sprinkle with cheese. Cover and bake approx. 30 minutes or until hot.
Parmesan cheese (to taste)	

Per serving (¼th)

Calories:	426
Protein:	25 g
Fat:	19 g
Cholesterol:	123 mg
Carbohydrates:	34 g
Sodium:	396 mg

Baked Penne with Mushrooms and Cheese

The variety of cheeses and mushrooms baked in a creamy sauce over this pasta makes for a delicious entrée.

Ovenproof baking dish
Preheat oven to 400°F
Serves 4–6

12 oz. penne pasta	Cook in boiling water until al dente (firm to the bite). Drain and set aside.
3 tbsp. butter **3 garlic cloves, crushed** **pinch of crushed red pepper** **1 lb. mushrooms, sliced thin** **(preferably wild)**	Combine and sauté mushrooms over medium heat for about 3 minutes. Set aside.
6 oz. Swiss cheese, grated **6 oz. soft mild cheese, grated** **(Havarti, brick or Bel Paese)** **¹/₃ cup Parmesan cheese**	Combine cheeses and set aside.
1 cup heavy cream	Set aside.
	Cover the bottom of the baking dish with a layer of pasta. Spread one-fourth of the mushroom and cheese mixtures over top. Repeat layering until mixtures have been used. Pour over the cream, sprinkle with ground pepper, and cover with foil. Bake, covered, for 12 minutes. Bake, uncovered, for another 12 minutes or until a light brown crust has formed on top. Serve.

Per serving (⅙th)	
Calories:	566
Protein:	25 g
Fat:	28 g
Cholesterol:	82 mg
Carbohydrates:	50 g
Sodium:	703 mg

Tortellini with Walnut Pesto

Walnut pesto is as good if not better than basil pesto. Use this sauce over any pasta of your choice.

Serves 4

1 lb. cheese-and-spinach-filled pasta (tortellini, ravioli, agnolotti)	Cook in boiling water until al dente (firm to the bite). Drain and set aside. Meanwhile, prepare sauce.
4 oz. walnuts* **1 tsp. crushed garlic** **¼ cup Romano or Parmesan cheese**	Grind in a food processor until mixture is well blended.
1 cup heavy cream	Heat in saucepan. Add above walnut mixture, combine, and cook for 1–2 minutes. Add pasta and toss with sauce. Serve.
½ cup sun-dried tomatoes, sliced thin	Garnish pasta with tomatoes.

*Toasting the nuts will give a better flavor. Toast in oven at 400°F or on top of stove in skillet until golden brown.

Per serving (¼th)	
Calories:	420
Protein:	8 g
Fat:	40 g
Cholesterol:	80 mg
Carbohydrates:	9 g
Sodium:	128 mg

Pine Nut Cannelloni*

Pine nuts and ricotta cheese make a delicious filling for any stuffed type of pasta.

Preheat oven to 350°F
Serves 4–6

approx. 10–12 cannelloni shells or manicotti shells	Cook in boiling water until al dente (firm to the bite). Drain, rinse, and set aside.

Filling

1/2 cup pine nuts	Toast in saucepan or oven at 400°F just until light brown.
1 1/4 cups ricotta cheese ***1/3 cup Parmesan cheese*** ***1/2 tsp. chopped sage*** ***(1/8 tsp. dry)*** ***salt and pepper to taste***	Mix well and add pine nuts. Place approx. 1 tbsp. in shells and place in baking pan side by side.

Sauce

4 tbsp. butter	Heat in skillet until medium brown. Remove from heat to cool. Set aside.
1 tbsp. butter ***1 small diced onion***	Sauté until onion is soft.
1 tbsp. sweet wine (sherry) ***1/2 cup chicken stock*** ***1/3 cup heavy cream***	Add to onions along with above browned butter. Cook for 3 minutes. Strain and pour sauce over cannelloni. Cook and bake until hot, approx. 25 minutes.

*This filling can be used to make other stuffed pastas such as ravioli, tortellini, etc. See page 10.

Per serving (1/6th)	
Calories:	397
Protein:	13 g
Fat:	28 g
Cholesterol:	66 mg
Carbohydrates:	25 g
Sodium:	388 mg

Stuffed Pasta with Gorgonzola Cream Sauce

The blue cheese remains very mild in this sauce.

Serves 4

1 lb. stuffed pasta such as ravioli, tortellini, or agnolotti (preferably stuffed with cheese mixture)	Cook in boiling water until firm to the bite (al dente). Drain and set aside. Meanwhile, prepare sauce.
3/4 cup heavy cream **4 oz. Gorgonzola (blue) cheese, cut into pieces**	In large saucepan, combine over medium heat until cheese is melted. Cook for 3 minutes. Add stuffed pasta and sauté in sauce for 2–3 minutes.
1/2 cup Parmesan cheese	Add to above and mix well.
3 slices prosciutto	Chop coarsely and serve over top individual pasta dishes.
1 tsp. chopped parsley	Sprinkle over top and serve.

Per serving (¼th)	
Calories:	513
Protein:	24 g
Fat:	35 g
Cholesterol:	208 mg
Carbohydrates:	25 g
Sodium:	1462 mg

Lamb Cannelloni with Walnut Parmesan Sauce

This delicate lamb filling is ideal for homemade stuffed pasta such as ravioli or tortellini.

Preheat oven to 375°F
Serves 4–6

12 dry cannelloni shells (or fresh made from lasagna sheets 5″ × 4″)	Cook in boiling water until just barely cooked (al dente). Drain and rinse with cold water and set aside.

Filling

1 tbsp. olive oil **½ medium onion, diced** **1 tsp. chopped garlic** **1 tbsp. fresh chopped rosemary (1 tsp. dry)** **½ lb. lamb, cut into cubes**	Heat oil in skillet. Add ingredients and cook until lamb is medium done.
2 tbsp. chopped parsley (1½ tsp. dry) **salt and pepper to taste**	Add and let cook slightly.
1 egg **¼ cup bread crumbs (preferably seasoned)**	Add to above and purée in food processor. Place approx. 1 heaping tbsp. into cannelloni shells. Place in baking dish.

Sauce

2 tbsp. butter **1 cup heavy cream** **2 tsp. chopped parsley** **2 tbsp. Parmesan cheese** **2 tsp. finely chopped walnuts (preferably toasted)**	Bring ingredients to a boil and pour over cannelloni shells. Cook and bake, covered, for approx. 15 minutes, just until hot.

Per serving (⅙th)

Calories:	396
Protein:	15 g
Fat:	25 g
Cholesterol:	136 mg
Carbohydrates:	28 g
Sodium:	198 mg

Ricotta-Stuffed Pasta Shells with Mushroom Sauce

The mushroom sauce highlights this light cheese-stuffed pasta.

Preheat oven to 375°F
1 large baking dish
Serves 4–6

16 jumbo pasta shells	Cook in boiling water until firm to the bite (al dente). Rinse with cold water and set aside. Meanwhile, prepare filling.
1 tbsp. olive oil **2 green onions, sliced thin** **1 bunch watercress leaves**	Heat in skillet until vegetables are wilted. Cool and chop finely.
1 lb. ricotta cheese **1 egg** **1 tbsp. freshly chopped parsley** **(1½ tsp. dry)** **salt and pepper to taste**	Add to above and mix until well-combined. Fill pasta shells with filling and place in baking dish. Prepare sauce.

Sauce

2 cups beef or veal stock (consommé)	Boil until reduced to 1 cup, approx. 5 minutes.
1½ cups sliced mushrooms (preferably wild, such as shiitake) **⅓ tsp. thyme or 2 fresh sprigs** **2 leaves chopped basil (½ tsp. dry)** **4 tsp. grated Romano or Parmesan cheese**	Add to stock and boil for 1 minute. Pour around stuffed shells in dish. Cover and bake for approx. 20 minutes or until hot.

Per serving (1/6th)

Calories:	410
Protein:	22 g
Fat:	15 g
Cholesterol:	104 mg
Carbohydrates:	45 g
Sodium:	719 mg

Tortellini with Creamy Cheese Sauce

*Mascarpone cheese is heavenly in this
pasta, but cream cheese or ricotta
will be as good.*

Serves 4

**¾ lb. stuffed cheese and
spinach pasta (tortellini,
agnolotti, ravioli, etc.)**

Cook in boiling water until al
dente (firm to the bite). Drain
and set aside.

Sauce

1 cup heavy cream

Bring to a boil.

**2 tbsp. butter
3 tbsp. Parmesan cheese
4 tbsp. mascarpone cheese
(or ricotta or cream cheese)
salt and pepper (white)
pinch of nutmeg**

Add these ingredients and boil
2 more minutes, stirring often.

Add pasta, toss, and serve.

Per serving (¼th)
Calories: 492
Protein: 14 g
Fat: 37 g
Cholesterol: 219 mg
Carbohydrates: 26 g
Sodium: 833 mg

Pasta Salad with Black Olives and Feta Cheese
City Restaurant,
Los Angeles

*Lasagna with Bell
Peppers, Eggplant,
and Zucchini*
Locanda Veneta, Los Angeles

Rigatoni with
Roasted Tomato Sauce
Anthony's, Houston

*Penne with Bell
Peppers, Mushrooms,
and Cheese*
Scoozi, Chicago

Pasta Filled with Chicken and Ricotta Cheese

Chicken, spinach, and ricotta cheese make a delectable filling for any stuffed pasta.

Preheat oven to 350°F
Serves 4–6

12–16 jumbo pasta shells (conchiglie)	Cook in boiling water until al dente (firm to the bite). Drain and set aside. Meanwhile, prepare sauce.
6 oz. raw chicken breast 1 tbsp. olive oil	Sauté until done. Cut into small pieces and set aside.
⅓ cup well-packed chopped spinach (frozen and defrosted)	Cook for 2 minutes in boiling water. Drain and squeeze out moisture.
1½ cups ricotta cheese 1 tbsp. chopped parsley 2 eggs salt and pepper	Add to spinach and chicken and mix well. Place approx. 1 tbsp. in shells and place in baking dish.
1 cup prepared tomato sauce or mascarpone sauce (see page 146)	Pour sauce over top, cover, and bake approx. 30 minutes or until hot.

Per serving (1/6th)

Calories:	271
Protein:	20 g
Fat:	9 g
Cholesterol:	127 mg
Carbohydrates:	24 g
Sodium:	230 mg

Seafood Cannelloni

A lot of ingredients and a little effort
makes this an outstanding stuffed pasta.

Preheat oven to 350°F
Serves 4–6

12 cannelloni shells or fresh pasta sheets 4" × 5"	Cook in boiling water until firm to the bite (al dente). Rinse in cold water to prevent sticking. Drain and set aside.
3 tbsp. olive oil **1/2 medium chopped onion** **2 cloves crushed garlic** **1/2 lb. white type of fish, cut into small pieces** **(cod, snapper, sea bass, etc.)**	Sauté onions and garlic until onions are soft. Add fish and cook for 1 minute.
3/4 tbsp. licorice liqueur **3 tbsp. white wine** **1/2 tbsp. lemon juice** **1/3 tbsp. mustard**	Add and cook approx. 2 minutes. Remove from heat.
2 oz. crabmeat **1 oz. baby shrimp** **4 tbsp. soft butter** **1/2 tsp. Worcestershire sauce** **4 oz. cooked chopped spinach, squeeze out moisture**	Fold into above and process just until large pieces are still evident. Stuff pasta shells and place in baking dish.
1 cup white or bechamel sauce (see page 15) **1 cup prepared tomato sauce**	Pour white sauce then tomato sauce over cannelloni.
1/2 cup Parmesan cheese	Sprinkle over tomato sauce. Cover and bake at 350°F for 25 minutes, until hot.

Per serving (¼th)

Calories:	404
Protein:	21 g
Fat:	23 g
Cholesterol:	85 mg
Carbohydrates:	25 g
Sodium:	429 mg

Pasta Rolls Filled with Smoked Salmon and Cheese

Manicotti shells filled with chopped spinach, cottage cheese, and smoked salmon topped with tomato sauce and melted cheese.

Preheat oven to 350°F
Large baking dish
Serves 4–5

10 manicotti shells	Cook in boiling water just until firm to the bite (al dente). Drain, rinse, and set aside.
1¼ cups cottage or ricotta cheese * ***4 oz. cooked spinach (well-drained)*** ***4 oz. smoked salmon, chopped*** ***pepper to taste***	Combine in bowl until well-mixed. Fill pasta shells.
2 cups tomato sauce	Pour 1 cup into baking dish. Lay manicotti over top. Pour remaining sauce over pasta.
½ cup grated Swiss cheese (preferably Gruyère)	Sprinkle over pasta. Cover and bake approx. 25 minutes, until hot.

*Ricotta cheese will give a creamier texture.

Per serving (⅕th)	
Calories:	303
Protein:	19 g
Fat:	10 g
Cholesterol:	36 mg
Carbohydrates:	31 g
Sodium:	1769 mg

Cheese and Pumpkin Cannelloni*

*The pumpkin gives this filling
a sweet and rich taste.*

Preheat oven to 350°F
Serves 4–6

12 cannelloni or manicotti shells — Cook in boiling water until firm to the bite (al dente). Drain in cold water and set aside. Meanwhile, prepare sauce.

**2 tbsp. olive oil
4 tbsp. butter** — Heat in skillet.

1 medium onion, chopped — Sauté until onions become golden brown. Remove from stove and set aside.

**½ lb. pumpkin, mashed (canned)
⅓ cup Parmesan cheese
4 oz. mascarpone cheese (or ricotta or cream cheese)
2 amaretti cookies, finely crushed, or crushed graham crackers
½ tbsp. bread crumbs** — Mix well and add to onion mixture. Place approx. 1 tbsp. into pasta shells, and place side by side in baking dish.

Sauce

**4 tbsp. melted butter
8 sage leaves (½ tsp. dry)
¼ cup heavy cream** — Combine in saucepan over medium heat just until boiling. Pour over shells, cover, and bake approx. 20 minutes or until hot.

*Homemade stuffed pasta can be made using this filling, such as ravioli, tortellini, etc. See page 10.

Per serving (⅙th)	
Calories:	397
Protein:	9 g
Fat:	28 g
Cholesterol:	67 mg
Carbohydrates:	28 g
Sodium:	304 mg

146

Ravioli with Nutty Cream Sauce

*Any combination of your favorite nuts
will be delicious in this creamy sauce.*

Serves 3–4

¼ cup hazelnuts *
2 tbsp. walnuts
⅓ cup pine nuts

Use these amounts or any combination you like and finely chop all nuts. Set aside.

¾ lb. ravioli (or tortellini)

Cook in boiling water until al dente (firm to the bite). Drain and set aside. Meanwhile, prepare sauce.

2 tbsp. butter
¾ cup heavy cream

Heat in saucepan.

salt and pepper to taste

Add along with half the nut mixture and cook just until boiling. Add pasta and toss.

¼ cup Parmesan cheese

Sprinkle with cheese and remaining nuts.

*Toasting these nuts will produce a more distinct flavor. Toast either on top of the stove or in a 400°F oven just until golden.

Per serving (¼th)

Calories:	524
Protein:	16 g
Fat:	45 g
Cholesterol:	167 mg
Carbohydrates:	19 g
Sodium:	291 mg

Tortellini with Prosciutto and Peas

A creamy cheese sauce highlighted with chopped ham and peas is delicious over any stuffed pasta.

Serves 4–6

1 lb. meat or cheese tortellini (or any stuffed pasta)	Cook in boiling water until al dente (firm to the bite). Drain and set aside. Meanwhile, prepare sauce.
4 tbsp. butter	Heat in large saucepan.
4 slices chopped prosciutto (or ham)	Add and sauté until lightly browned. Add pasta.
1 cup heavy cream **1/2 cup cooked green peas** **1/2 cup Parmesan cheese** **salt and pepper**	Add and stir on medium heat just until well-mixed. Serve.

Per serving (1/6th)

Calories:	405
Protein:	16 g
Fat:	31 g
Cholesterol:	169 mg
Carbohydrates:	16 g
Sodium:	515 mg

Pasta with Basic Sauces

Bow Tie Pasta with Creamy Tomato Sauce

Green peas in a creamy tomato sauce highlighted with spicy Italian sausage.

Serves 2–4

½ lb. bow tie pasta (farfalle or any wide, flat noodle)	Cook in boiling water until al dente (firm to the bite). Drain and set aside. Meanwhile, prepare sauce.
4 oz. medium spicy sausage	Peel skin off sausages and slice. Cook in large skillet, crumbling with a fork, until brown.
4 tbsp. butter ***½ cup heavy cream*** ***½ cup green peas*** ***½ cup prepared tomato sauce***	Add to above sausage and cook until a boil is reached.
¼ cup Parmesan cheese	Add to sauce to thicken, then add pasta and toss. Serve with more Parmesan if desired.

Per serving (¼th)	
Calories:	580
Protein:	14 g
Fat:	37 g
Cholesterol:	147 mg
Carbohydrates:	46 g
Sodium:	493 mg

Penne with Pomodoro Sauce

*A light, yet rich and creamy
tomato-based sauce.*

Serves 2–4

½ lb. penne (short pasta tubes)	Cook in boiling water until al dente (firm to the bite). Drain and set aside. Meanwhile, prepare sauce.
Pomodoro Sauce	
2 tbsp. olive oil	Heat in large saucepan.
1 tsp. minced garlic	Add and sauté 1 minute.
1 cup finely chopped tomatoes (preferably Roma) *1 tbsp. minced basil (½ tsp. dry)* *salt and pepper to taste*	Add and simmer 10 minutes. Set sauce aside.
2 tbsp. olive oil	Heat in skillet.
3 oz. bacon, chopped (preferably Italian pancetta) *2 garlic cloves, crushed* *½ tsp. oregano*	Add and sauté until garlic turns golden and bacon is partially cooked. (You can pour off excess oil or keep for sauce.)
2 tbsp. white wine	Add and stir. Add above tomato sauce and simmer for 3 minutes.
4 tbsp. butter	Add to sauce along with pasta and toss.
¼ cup Parmesan cheese	Serve with cheese.

Per serving (¼th)	
Calories:	592
Protein:	11 g
Fat:	40 g
Cholesterol:	51 mg
Carbohydrates:	45 g
Sodium:	428 mg

Capellini with Tomatoes and Basil Sauce

A simple dish with Roma tomatoes, basil, and garlic.

Serves 4–6

1 lb. thin pasta (angel hair, capellini, spaghettini)	Cook in boiling water until al dente (firm to the bite). Drain and set aside. Meanwhile, prepare sauce.
1¹/₂ lbs. chopped tomatoes (preferably Roma) **1 clove crushed garlic** **6 leaves chopped basil (1 tsp. dry)** **salt and pepper to taste** **¹/₂ cup olive oil**	Combine in bowl.
2 tbsp. olive oil	Heat in large saucepan. Add above tomato mixture and heat thoroughly. Add pasta and toss until mixture is hot and well-combined.
¹/₄ cup Parmesan cheese	Serve with cheese and basil leaves as a garnish.

Per serving (¹/₆th)	
Calories:	518
Protein:	12 g
Fat:	25 g
Cholesterol:	2 mg
Carbohydrates:	62 g
Sodium:	110 mg

Rigatoni with Roasted Tomato Sauce

Tomatoes broiled, charred, and puréed
are outstanding over rigatoni.

Preheat oven to broil
Serves 4–6

1 lb. rigatoni pasta	Cook in boiling water until al dente (firm to the bite). Drain and set aside. Meanwhile, prepare sauce.
8–10 small tomatoes (preferably Roma)	Broil or grill tomatoes until black on the outside, approx. 15 minutes. Do not peel. Place in blender and purée. Set aside.
2 tbsp. olive oil	Heat in large skillet.
1 tbsp. crushed garlic	Sauté until light brown.
1/2 cup sliced mushrooms **1/4 cup green peas**	Add to garlic and sauté until mushrooms are cooked. Add tomato purée and cook for 3 minutes.
salt and pepper to taste **1/4 cup chopped basil** **(2 tsp. dry)** **1/4 cup Parmesan cheese**	Add, combine, and add pasta. Toss and serve.

Per serving (1/6th)

Calories:	356
Protein:	12 g
Fat:	6 g
Cholesterol:	2 mg
Carbohydrates:	61 g
Sodium:	121 mg

154

Capellini with Tomato Basil Sauce

A simple pasta to accompany a hearty meal.

Serves 4–6

1 lb. capellini (or any thin pasta)
Cook in boiling water until al dente (firm to the bite). Drain and set aside. Meanwhile, prepare sauce.

⅓ cup olive oil
Heat in large skillet.

3 crushed garlic cloves
2 tbsp. finely chopped onion
Sauté for 2 minutes.

1½ lbs. fresh tomatoes, diced
Add and continue cooking until tomatoes become soft, approx. 5 minutes.

6 chopped basil leaves (1 tsp. dry)
salt and pepper
Add to sauce and stir. Add pasta and mix well.

Parmesan cheese to taste

Per serving (⅙th)	
Calories:	400
Protein:	12 g
Fat:	12 g
Cholesterol:	2 mg
Carbohydrates:	62 g
Sodium:	112 mg

Basic Tomato Sauce

A simple sauce that can be an accompaniment for any pasta.

Serves 4
Serve over any type of pasta desired (approx. 1 lb.)

3 tbsp. olive oil **1 small onion, finely chopped** **2 garlic cloves, crushed** **1 stalk of celery, finely chopped** **1 carrot, finely chopped**	In large frying pan, cook until vegetables become soft.
⅓ cup dry white wine	Add to above and cook for approx. 2–4 minutes.
1 can (28-oz.) tomatoes, including juice (preferably Italian plum)	Add and cook on medium heat for 30 minutes, uncovered. Stir, occasionally breaking tomatoes with the back of a spoon.

Per serving (¼th)	
Calories:	141
Protein:	2 g
Fat:	10 g
Cholesterol:	0 mg
Carbohydrates:	10 g
Sodium:	290 mg

Pasta Puttanara

A spicy tomato sauce.

Serves 4

³/₄ lb. fettuccine	Cook in boiling water until al dente (firm to the bite). Drain and set aside. Meanwhile, prepare sauce.
2 tbsp. butter *2 tbsp. olive oil*	Heat in large saucepan.
1 stalk celery, finely diced *¹/₂ small carrot, finely diced* *¹/₂ small onion, finely diced*	Add and cook on medium heat until vegetables are soft, approx. 5 minutes.
¹/₄ tsp. dry basil *salt and pepper to taste* *1 oz. sliced black olives* *1 oz. sliced green olives* *1 anchovy, minced* *1 tsp. capers or to taste*	Add and cook 1 minute.
16 oz. tomatoes (canned with liquid or fresh) *1 tbsp. tomato paste*	Purée tomatoes, add to above, and simmer 15–20 minutes, stirring occasionally. Add pasta and toss.
chopped parsley and croutons for garnish	

Per serving (¹/₄th)	
Calories:	476
Protein:	12 g
Fat:	16 g
Cholesterol:	16 mg
Carbohydrates:	71 g
Sodium:	615 mg

Rigatoni in Red Wine Sauce

A simple dish that can accompany any entrée.

Serves 4

1 cup red wine (preferably Barolo)	Boil in large saucepan approx. 4 minutes, or until reduced to almost half.
¹/₂ chopped onion **2 small sprigs of thyme** **(¹/₂ tsp. dry)** **2 cups prepared tomato sauce**	Add to above and simmer for another 15 minutes. In the meantime, cook the pasta.
³/₄ lb. rigatoni	Cook in boiling water until al dente (firm to the bite). Drain, add to the sauce, and serve.

Per serving (¹/₄th)	
Calories:	349
Protein:	12 g
Fat:	1 g
Cholesterol:	0 mg
Carbohydrates:	70 g
Sodium:	163 mg

Risottos

Risotto with Fresh Spring Vegetables

Italian rice with fresh, crisp
vegetables in a tomato sauce.

Serves 4–6

2 cups fresh spring vegetables (combination of zucchini, eggplant, bell peppers, mushrooms, etc.)	Cut up vegetables and cook for 1 minute in boiling water. Drain and set aside.
¼ cup butter	Melt in medium pan.
8 oz. rice (preferably Italian risotto)	Add and sauté until light brown, approx. 5 minutes.
Approx. 3 cups chicken broth **1 cup tomato sauce**	Add slowly to rice and stir often until all the liquid is absorbed, approx. 20–25 minutes. Add drained vegetables.
salt and pepper to taste **¼ cup of Parmesan cheese**	Add, mix, and serve.

Per serving (⅙th)

Calories:	246
Protein:	4 g
Fat:	10 g
Cholesterol:	26 mg
Carbohydrates:	33 g
Sodium:	791 mg

Risotto with Mushrooms, Onions, and Brandy

A touch of brandy adds incredible flavor to this risotto dish.

Serves 4–6

³/₄ lb. mushrooms (preferably wild such as oyster, chanterelle, etc.)	Chop and reserve.
2 tbsp. butter *2 tbsp. olive oil*	Heat over medium heat in medium saucepan.
1 large diced onion *¹/₂ tbsp. crushed garlic* *salt and pepper*	Add and cook until onions are golden. Add above chopped mushrooms and sauté until soft.
¹/₄ cup brandy	Add, turn heat to high, and stir.
8 oz. rice (preferably Italian risotto)	Add rice and sauté until light brown, approx. 5 minutes.
1 bay leaf *approx. 3 cups chicken stock* *(canned is fine)*	Add slowly and cook on a medium heat for approx. 15 minutes, stirring often so rice does not stick. Add as much broth as required until rice is done.
¹/₂ cup Parmesan cheese or to taste	Add, toss, and serve.

Per serving (¹/₆th)

Calories:	275
Protein:	6 g
Fat:	10 g
Cholesterol:	16 mg
Carbohydrates:	35 g
Sodium:	679 mg

Risotto with Sweet Sausage and Vegetables

Italian rice with crisp bacon and sweet sausage is a great combination.

Serves 4–6

1 tsp. olive oil *4 tbsp. butter*	Heat in medium-sized skillet.
1 small onion, chopped *1 small carrot, diced* *1 celery stalk, diced* *2 oz. bacon, chopped* *(preferably Italian pancetta)*	Add and sauté until vegetables become soft.
6 oz. sweet (mild) sausage	Remove skin, chop, and add to above, cooking until almost done on a medium heat. (Use a fork to crumble.)
8 oz. rice *(preferably Italian risotto)*	Add to above and sauté just until light brown.
approx. 3½ cups beef broth *(consommé)*	On moderate heat, add slowly to above, stirring often, until all the liquid has been absorbed, approx. 20–25 minutes. Remove from heat.
¼ cup Parmesan cheese	Add to above and serve hot.

Per serving (⅙th)

Calories:	415
Protein:	8 g
Fat:	26 g
Cholesterol:	50 mg
Carbohydrates:	32 g
Sodium:	959 mg

Risotto with Pine Nuts and Spinach

*This buttery rice is enhanced with
cheese, spinach, and pine nuts.*

Serves 4–6

¾ lb. chopped spinach (fresh or frozen)	Cook in boiling water until done. Squeeze out moisture. Set aside.
⅓ cup pine nuts	Toast in skillet or oven at 400°F until lightly browned. Set aside.
2 tbsp. butter 1 tbsp. oil	Heat in medium pan.
2 tbsp. finely chopped onion	Add and cook until soft.
1 cup rice (preferably Italian risotto)	Add and sauté for 2 minutes.
3 cups chicken stock	Add slowly and cook on a medium heat, stirring often, until all liquid is absorbed, approx. 15–20 minutes. Add spinach and pine nuts. Remove from heat.
¼ cup Parmesan cheese	Add to above and serve.

Per serving (⅙th)

Calories: 438

Protein: 14 g

Fat: 23 g

Cholesterol: 20 mg

Carbohydrates: 47 g

Sodium: 928 mg

Risotto Fiorentina

*Italian rice with ground beef
and white wine.*

Serves 4–6

2 tbsp. olive oil **1 tbsp. butter**	Heat in medium-sized saucepan.
1 tbsp. chopped parsley **(1 tsp. dry)** **1 tbsp. chopped carrot** **1 tbsp. chopped celery** **1 tbsp. chopped basil** **(½ tsp. dry)**	Add and cook for 3 minutes on a medium heat.
4 oz. ground beef	Add and cook for 5–8 minutes, until just cooked.
4 tbsp. white wine	Add and cook for 2 more minutes.
8 oz. rice (preferably Italian risotto)	Add and stir until light brown.
approx. 3½ cups beef stock (consommé)	Add slowly, stirring constantly. Cook for approx. 20–25 minutes on a medium-low heat, until liquid is absorbed by rice.
⅓ cup Parmesan cheese	Add just before serving.

Per serving (⅙th)

Calories: 394
Protein: 13 g
Fat: 15 g
Cholesterol: 34 mg
Carbohydrates: 47 g
Sodium: 1016 mg

Italian Rice with Spring Vegetables

Rice with crisp vegetables
and chopped ham.

Serves 4–6

1 medium zucchini, diced *4 asparagus spears,* *chopped* *6 mushrooms, sliced* *½ cup broccoli, chopped* *½ cup cauliflower, chopped*	Steam or cook in boiling water just until crisp for 5 minutes. Set aside.
2 tbsp. olive oil	Heat in large skillet.
1 medium onion, chopped *4 slices prosciutto (or ham),* *chopped*	Add and sauté until golden brown.
8 oz. rice (preferably *Italian risotto)*	Add to pan and stir for 2 minutes.
½ cup white wine *approx. 3 cups chicken or* *beef stock*	Add slowly to rice, stirring often, on a medium-low heat until liquid is absorbed, approx. 20 minutes.
1 medium tomato, chopped	Add to above rice along with cooked vegetables and stir well.
½ cup Parmesan cheese	Add cheese, toss, and serve immediately.

Per serving (⅙th)

Calories:	390
Protein:	13 g
Fat:	12 g
Cholesterol:	12 mg
Carbohydrates:	56 g
Sodium:	1040 mg

Mushroom and Chicken Risotto

A simple rice dish highlighted with
morsels of chicken and mushrooms.

Serves 4

2 tbsp. olive oil **1 tbsp. finely chopped** **shallots or onions** **¹/₂ cup sliced mushrooms**	In medium skillet, sauté for 2–4 minutes.
8 oz. rice. (preferably **Italian risotto)**	Add and cook for another 3 minutes. Do not let rice brown.
¹/₂ cup white wine **approx. 2¹/₂ cups chicken** **broth**	Add slowly to rice and cook on a medium heat for approx. 15–20 minutes, until liquid is absorbed and rice is tender. (Add more broth if needed.)
4 tbsp. butter **1 tbsp. Parmesan cheese** **3 oz. diced cooked chicken**	Add to rice, stir, and serve.

Per serving (¹/₄th)

Calories:	432
Protein:	10 g
Fat:	21 g
Cholesterol:	47 mg
Carbohydrates:	47 g
Sodium:	844 mg

Linguine Salad with Brie Cheese and Tomatoes

The soft and mild Brie cheese melts gently over this tomato and sweet onion pasta dish.

Serves 4–6

1lb. tomatoes, cut into cubes
8 oz. Brie cheese (or Camembert) diced
½ cup chopped basil (1 tbsp. dry)
½ sweet onion, sliced thin
2 tsp. chopped garlic
1 cup olive oil
¼ cup Parmesan cheese

Mix together in large bowl to marinate. Meanwhile, prepare pasta.

1 lb. linguine

Cook in boiling water until al dente (firm to the bite). Drain and immediately toss with above mixture. Serve cold.

(This pasta tastes best if left to marinate for 1–2 hours.)

Per serving (⅙th)	
Calories:	449
Protein:	19 g
Fat:	13 g
Cholesterol:	29 mg
Carbohydrates:	62 g
Sodium:	378 mg

Pasta Salad with Black Olives and Feta Cheese

A wonderful cold pasta salad resembling a Greek salad.

Serves 4–6

¾ lb. small shell pasta or tubes

Cook in boiling water until al dente (firm to the bite). Drain and rinse.

¼ cup olive oil

Add to pasta, toss, and set aside. Meanwhile, prepare dressing.

½ cup olive oil
8 oz. crumbled feta cheese
¾ cup black olives
2 medium diced tomatoes
1 large red onion, sliced
3 small cucumbers, * peeled and diced (preferably pickling or kirbies)
1 small bunch chopped oregano (1½ tbsp. dry)
salt and pepper to taste
dash of Tabasco (optional)

Combine in large bowl and add pasta. Chill and serve.

* If these small cucumbers are not available, use 2 small regular cucumbers.

Per serving (⅙th)	
Calories:	642
Protein:	17 g
Fat:	41 g
Cholesterol:	39 mg
Carbohydrates:	49 g
Sodium:	1126 mg

172

Chilled Penne Tomato Salad

*A light, refreshing pasta salad
for lunch or side dish.*

Serves 4

**³/₄ lb. penne pasta
(short tubes)**

Cook in boiling water until al dente (firm to the bite). Drain and set aside. Meanwhile, prepare sauce.

**1 lb. fresh tomatoes, diced
¹/₂ cup chopped basil
(1 tbsp. dry)
1 yellow pepper, thinly
sliced
¹/₂ cup olive oil
2 crushed garlic cloves
salt and pepper to taste**

Combine in large bowl, add pasta, toss, and allow to chill and marinate for at least 1–2 hours.

Per serving (¹/₄th)
Calories: 590
Protein: 12 g
Fat: 28 g
Cholesterol: 4 mg
Carbohydrates: 72 g
Sodium: 69 mg

Gnocchi with Meat Sauce

*This is a hearty and
rich-tasting pasta dish.*

Serves 4–5

1 lb. gnocchi (use either packaged or see page 179)	Cook in boiling water until firm to the bite (al dente). Drain and set aside.
3 tbsp. oil	Heat oil in large saucepan.
1 medium onion, finely chopped **1 celery stalk, finely chopped** **1 carrot, finely chopped** **2 garlic cloves, finely chopped** **$^1/_2$ tsp. rosemary, chopped ($^1/_4$ tsp. dry)** **$^1/_3$ cup chopped mushrooms**	Add and sauté until vegetables are soft.
8 oz. ground beef **4 oz. finely chopped ham** **4 oz. finely chopped chicken livers**	Add and cook until meat is lightly browned. (Drain off excess oil, if desired.)
1 tbsp. flour	Stir into above until well-blended.
$^1/_2$ cup red wine	Add and cook over medium heat for approx. 20 minutes, stirring occasionally. Pour over gnocchi.

Per serving (⅕th)

Calories:	520
Protein:	27 g
Fat:	24 g
Cholesterol:	185 mg
Carbohydrates:	43 g
Sodium:	395 mg

Potato Mushroom Gnocchi

*An interesting version of gnocchi
enhanced with fresh herbs. Serve with
one of your favorite sauces.*

*Makes 2 lbs. of gnocchi
Serves 6–8*

4 cups cooked diced potato (approx. 1¼ lbs.)

Purée until no lumps are evident. Set aside.

4 tbsp. olive oil

Heat in skillet.

**1 tbsp. finely cut mushrooms (preferably wild)
1 tbsp. finely cut parsley
1 tsp. finely cut rosemary (¼ tsp. dry)
1 tsp. finely cut basil (½ tsp. dry)
salt and pepper**

Add and sauté mushrooms and herbs for approx. 2–4 minutes. Add to potato and combine.

approx. 2¼ cups flour

Add slowly to above on a floured surface and knead until dough is no longer sticky, approx. 5 minutes. Add more flour if necessary. Cut in 4 pieces and roll out each into long, narrow rolls. Cut into ½" pieces. Cook gnocchi in a large pan of boiling water until they rise to the top, approx. 3–4 minutes. Cook in batches. Remove with a slotted spoon and serve with sauce of your choice.

(Cut pieces can be frozen and cooked later. No need to defrost.)

Per serving (⅛th)	
Calories:	240
Protein:	4 g
Fat:	7 g
Cholesterol:	0 mg
Carbohydrates:	38 g
Sodium:	33 mg

Gnocchi (Potato Pasta Dumpling)

This is a delicious conventional recipe for gnocchi. Great with any sauce of your choice.

Serves 4

1 lb. white potatoes	Boil until potatoes are cooked, approx. 30–45 minutes. Peel and purée until the lumps disappear.
2 tbsp. butter	Melt butter in saucepan and add mashed potatoes and stir vigorously.
1 egg yolk	Add and stir quickly so egg cannot cook. Remove from stove. Place mixture on floured counter.
approx. 1 cup flour	Add slowly to potato mixture and knead as if bread for approx. 5 minutes. Add enough flour so that dough is not sticky. Divide dough into 4 pieces. Roll each out to ½" diameter and cut into ½" pieces. (Design gnocchi as you wish, i.e. thumbs or fork imprint.) Place in large pot of boiling water for approx. 4 minutes. Serve with tomato, pesto sauce, or sauce of your choice.

(Gnocchi can be frozen before cooking. Cut into pieces and leave out to dry approx. 1½ hours, then place in freezer bags.)

Per serving (¼th)

Calories:	283
Protein:	6 g
Fat:	8 g
Cholesterol:	84 mg
Carbohydrates:	46 g
Sodium:	70 mg

Spinach and Ricotta Dumplings

A delicate gnocchi.

Serves 2–4

**6 oz. cooked drained
spinach
(frozen is fine)
salt and pepper to taste
pinch nutmeg
1/2 tbsp. soft butter
1/2 cup ricotta cheese
1 egg
3 tbsp. Parmesan cheese
2 tbsp. flour**

Combine in food processor. In large pot of simmering water (not boiling water), drop by teaspoonfuls and cook just until they rise to the top, approx. 2–4 minutes. Carefully remove them with a slotted spoon and place in serving dish. (If handled too aggressively they may fall apart.) Serve with either prepared tomato sauce and grated Parmesan or the following sauce.

**Optional Butter
and Cheese Sauce**

**1/4 cup melted butter
1/4 cup Parmesan cheese**

Combine and pour over dumplings.

Per serving (¼th)	
Calories:	233
Protein:	9 g
Fat:	19 g
Cholesterol:	119 mg
Carbohydrates:	7 g
Sodium:	373 mg

Ricotta Dumplings

These resemble a gnocchi without the potatoes. Serve with tomato, pesto sauce, or any sauce of your choice.

Serves 2–4

2 egg yolks
8 oz. ricotta cheese
2¹⁄₂ tbsp. Parmesan cheese
salt and pepper

Combine in food processor. Place in bowl.

3¹⁄₂ tbsp. flour

Add to above and work into mixture.

2 egg whites

Beat until stiff in clean bowl and carefully fold into cheese mixture.

4 tbsp. bread crumbs

Add to above and combine gently. Form balls with a teaspoon and cook in a large saucepan of boiling water for approx. 2 minutes. Turn off heat and let dumplings sit in the pot covered for another 6 minutes. Carefully remove them from water with a slotted spoon and place on a plate covered with paper towels. Carefully pour off extra liquid and serve with prepared tomato sauce, or sauce of your choice.

Per serving (¹⁄₄th)
Calories: 185
Protein: 12 g
Fat: 8 g
Cholesterol: 158 mg
Carbohydrates: 13 g
Sodium: 260 mg

Crepes (Crespelle) with Ricotta Filling

*An outstanding Italian crepe filled
with a delicate cheese mixture.*

Preheat oven to 350°F
Makes approx. 10 crepes
Serves 4–5

Crepes

1¹/₂ cups milk **2 eggs** **1 cup flour**	Blend in processor.
2 tbsp. butter	Melt in 9″–10″ skillet and pour butter into batter. Using ¹/₄ cup measuring utensil, pour batter in pan, to form thin crepes. (If batter is too thick add a little more milk.) When brown on one side (approx. 1 minute), turn over and cook on other side an additional 30 seconds. Repeat with remaining batter. Set crepes aside.

Filling

¹/₄ cup chopped well-packed spinach **(if using fresh, use ¹/₂ cup)**	Cook in boiling water for a few minutes. Drain well and chop in blender or food processor. Place in bowl.
1 cup ricotta cheese **¹/₄ cup mascarpone cheese** **(or cream cheese or ricotta)** **¹/₄ cup Parmesan cheese** **1 egg yolk** **salt and pepper (white preferred)** **¹/₃ cup chopped prosciutto or ham**	Add to spinach and mix well. Place approx. 1 tbsp. onto each crepe and roll to form a tube. Cut the roll into small sections of approx. 1″ and place pieces vertically in a lightly buttered baking dish so the filling is visible.

(continued)

Per serving (¹/₅th)	
Calories:	467
Protein:	21 g
Fat:	29 g
Cholesterol:	243 mg
Carbohydrates:	28 g
Sodium:	626 mg

182

Crepes (Crespelle) with Ricotta Filling *(continued)*

Sauce

⅓ cup Parmesan cheese	Sprinkle with cheese.
¼ cup melted butter	Pour over crepes. Cover and bake until hot, approx. 20 minutes.

Crepes (Crespelle) Filled with Cheese and Spinach

An Italian crepe with a mix of cheese and spinach.

Preheat oven to 350°F
Makes approx. 10 crepes
Serves 4–5

Crepes

1½ cups milk *2 eggs* *1 cup flour*	Blend in processor.
2 tbsp. butter	Melt in skillet and pour into above batter. Pour approx. ¼–⅓ cup amounts of batter into skillet to form crepes. Cook on one side until done. Turn and cook briefly on other side. Repeat until all batter is used.

Filling

4 oz. goat cheese *2 oz. blue cheese* *(preferably Gorgonzola)* *8 oz. mozzarella cheese* *4 oz. spinach, cooked and drained well* *1 tbsp. soft butter*	Cut cheeses in cubes. Process all ingredients until well-blended. Spread approx. 2 tbsp. of mixture over entire crepe and roll tightly. Chill for approx. 20 minutes. Slice crepes as pinwheels approx. 1″ thick. Place in baking dish.
1½ cups prepared tomato sauce *2 tbsp. soft butter or* *2 tbsp. heavy cream* *⅓ cup Parmesan cheese*	Pour sauce over crepes. Place butter or cream over top tomato sauce. Sprinkle cheese over top, cover, and bake approx. 25 minutes or until hot.

Per serving (⅕th)	
Calories:	514
Protein:	27 g
Fat:	31 g
Cholesterol:	197 mg
Carbohydrates:	29 g
Sodium:	916 mg

Seasoned Fettuccine in Consommé Broth

*A simple fettuccine for a
side dish to a heavy dinner.*

Serves 2–4

½ lb. fettuccine	Cook in boiling salted water until firm to the bite (al dente). Drain and set aside. Meanwhile, prepare sauce.
4 tbsp. butter	Heat in large skillet.
½ chopped onion	Sauté until onions become soft.
⅛ tsp. black pepper *⅛ tsp. poultry seasoning* *⅛ tsp. thyme*	Add and mix.
1 cup consommé (beef stock)	Add to above before butter browns. Add cooked fettuccine and mix well with the sauce. Serve.

Per serving (¼th)

Calories:	327
Protein:	7 g
Fat:	12 g
Cholesterol:	32 mg
Carbohydrates:	44 g
Sodium:	360 mg

Capellini Frittata with Bacon and Peas

This is the most unusual pasta dish ever created! Similar to a cheese omelette, the pasta added gives it a very different taste and texture.

Serves 4–6

2 oz. capellini or any thin strand pasta	Break into 2″ pieces and cook in boiling water just until firm to the bite (al dente). Drain and set aside.
4 eggs **1 cup grated mozzarella cheese** **salt and pepper**	Combine in bowl. Add above pasta and mix well. Set aside.
6 thin slices of bacon (preferably Italian pancetta)	Cut into small pieces and sauté just until crisp. Set aside.
1 cup peas, lightly cooked **⅓ cup Parmesan cheese**	Combine in bowl with above bacon. Mix well. Set aside.
3 tbsp. olive oil **3 crushed garlic cloves**	Heat in large non-stick skillet and sauté garlic for 1 minute. Pour half the egg mixture into skillet, and pour the pea mixture over top. Top this with the remaining egg mixture. Cook on a medium heat for approx. 8 minutes. Carefully invert frittata onto a large platter and slide back into skillet. Cook on this other side for 5 more minutes or until golden brown. Serve warm or at room temperature.

Per serving (⅙th)	
Calories:	424
Protein:	23 g
Fat:	28 g
Cholesterol:	306 mg
Carbohydrates:	17 g
Sodium:	663 mg

186

Penne Marinara

A light, mildly spicy dish.

Serves 4

¹/₂ lb. penne pasta (short tubes)	Cook in boiling water until al dente (firm to the bite). Drain and set aside. Meanwhile, prepare sauce.
¹/₂ tbsp. olive oil	Heat in large saucepan.
¹/₂ cup diced onion	Sauté until tender.
1 tsp. crushed garlic *¹/₂ tbsp. chopped capers* *1 tsp. dry basil* *¹/₂ tsp. dry oregano* *1 bay leaf*	Add and cook briefly.
14 oz. chopped tomatoes *2¹/₂ oz. pitted black olives, sliced* *pepper to taste* *1¹/₂ tbsp. tomato paste*	Add and simmer, partially covered, 10–15 minutes, stirring occasionally. Add pasta and toss.
1¹/₂ tbsp. Parmesan cheese	Sprinkle and serve.

Per serving (¹/₄th)
Calories: 288
Protein: 9 g
Fat: 6 g
Cholesterol: 1 mg
Carbohydrates: 50 g
Sodium: 620 mg

Linguine Toscano

A traditional spicy Italian dish.

Serves 4

¹/₂ lb. linguine (preferably whole wheat)	Cook in boiling water until al dente (firm to the bite). Drain and set aside. Meanwhile, prepare sauce.
2 tsp. olive oil	Heat in large pan.
1 small onion, chopped 4 crushed garlic cloves	Sauté until onions are soft.
1 (14–16-oz.) can crushed tomatoes, with juice dash of cayenne pepper 2 tsp. dry oregano	Add and simmer, uncovered, 10–15 minutes.
2 medium tomatoes, cut into thin strips 6 black olives, sliced 2 tsp. Parmesan cheese	Add and cook 2 more minutes. Add pasta, toss, and serve.

Per serving (¹/₄th)

Calories:	282
Protein:	9 g
Fat:	5 g
Cholesterol:	6 mg
Carbohydrates:	51 g
Sodium:	322 mg

Stuffed Pasta with
Gorgonzola Cream
Sauce
La Sila, Montreal

*Fettuccine with Scallops
and Smoked Salmon*
Giuliano's, Carmel

*Whole Red Peppers
Stuffed with Capellini
and Prosciutto Ham*
Daniel's, Tucson

Angel Hair Pasta with
Tomato and Seafood
Palio, New York

Vegetable Lasagna

*A light and tasty lasagna with a
variety of vegetables and cheeses.*

Preheat oven to 350°F
9″ × 13″ baking pan
Serves 8

Approx. 9 sheets of lasagna (whole wheat if possible)	Cook in boiling water with 1 tbsp. oil, until al dente (firm to the bite). Drain, rinse, and set aside.
3 oz. mozzarella cheese	Grate and set aside.
4 cups prepared tomato sauce	Set aside.
12 oz. sliced zucchini	Steam until tender and set aside.
1 tsp. olive oil	Heat in skillet.
3 crushed garlic cloves ½ cup diced onion	Add and cook until onion is soft.
12 oz. chopped spinach (if frozen, defrost)	Add, cover, and steam until soft. Cook until all liquid has evaporated. Set aside.

(continued)

Per serving (⅛th)	
Calories:	210
Protein:	12 g
Fat:	4 g
Cholesterol:	8 mg
Carbohydrates:	33 g
Sodium:	331 mg

Vegetable Lasagna *(continued)*

1 cup ricotta cheese
³/₄ cup cottage cheese
2 tbsp. Parmesan cheese
1 tbsp. chopped chives or
green onions
1 egg white

Process ingredients until combined.

Assembly

Spread ¹/₃ of the tomato sauce on bottom of pan. Set down approx. 3 lasagnas. Spread half ricotta cheese mixture over top. Spread all of spinach mixture over top. Spread 1 cup of sauce over top. Top with 3 more lasagnas. Add remainder of ricotta mixture, all of the zucchini, and 1 more cup of sauce. Top with remaining lasagnas, scatter mozzarella over top, and pour remaining sauce over top. Bake, covered, for 45–60 minutes.

Vegetable Cannelloni with Cream Sauce

*Mixed vegetables stuffed into pasta shells served
with a cream sauce and garlic bread crumb topping.*

Preheat oven to 350°F
13" × 9" baking dish
Serves 8 (2 cannelloni per person)

**16 cannelloni shells or
lasagna sheets 5" × 4"**

Cook in boiling water until firm
to the bite (al dente). Rinse with
cold water and set aside. Meanwhile, prepare filling.

Spinach Filling

**1¼ cups finely diced onion
1¼ cups finely diced carrots**

Spray a large skillet with nonstick vegetable spray. Add
vegetables and sauté until soft-
ened, approx. 3 minutes.

**3 cloves crushed garlic
½ cup red or yellow pepper, diced
¾ lb. spinach (preferably fresh)**

Add to above and cook until
spinach has wilted. (Spinach
may have to be added in
2 stages.)

**4 oz. tofu crumbled
¼ tsp. salt
black pepper to taste
¼ tsp. liquid smoke (optional)
¼ cup Parmesan cheese**

Add to above and heat thoroughly. Fill the pasta shells with
stuffing and set aside. Meanwhile, prepare the following
sauce.

**1½ cups chicken stock
1 bay leaf
⅓ cup onion, finely diced
1 crushed garlic clove**

Reserve ½ cup stock. Place ingredients into saucepan; bring
to a boil, cover, and simmer 5
minutes. (Remove bay leaf.)
Pour into food processor. Add
reserved chicken stock. Process
until smooth. Return to
saucepan.

(continued)

Per serving (⅛th)
Calories: 282
Protein: 17 g
Fat: 4.1 g
Cholesterol: 6 g
Carbohydrates: 8 mg
Sodium: 361 mg

193

Vegetable Cannelloni with Cream Sauce *(continued)*

³/₄ cup evaporated milk (low fat)
1 ¹/₄ tbsp. flour
salt and pepper to taste
pinch of nutmeg

Add to above, heat until a simmer, stirring often, for approx. 5 minutes.

1 clove crushed garlic
¹/₃ cup Parmesan

Add to sauce until combined, and cook 2 more minutes. Set aside.

Garlic Bread Crumb Topping

¹/₂ tsp. oil
1 crushed garlic clove
¹/₄ cup bread crumbs

Heat in skillet and stir well, until lightly browned. Remove from heat.

1 tbsp. Parmesan cheese
1 tbsp. chopped parsley

Add and stir. Unused topping can be frozen for later use.

Assembly

Pour half the cream sauce in bottom of baking dish. Place stuffed cannelloni over top. Pour remaining sauce over top and sprinkle a little Parmesan cheese over top. Cover and bake for 20 minutes. Uncover and sprinkle approx. 2–3 tbsp. of the bread crumb topping. Bake another 10 minutes.

Lasagna with Ricotta Cheese and Tomato Sauce

A "light," old-fashioned lasagna.

Preheat oven to 300°F
Spray a 9″ × 13″ baking pan with
nonstick vegetable coating
Serves 8

Approx. 9–10 sheets of lasagna	Cook in boiling water until al dente (firm to the bite). Drain and set aside. Meanwhile, prepare sauce.
8 oz. mozzarella cheese, grated	Set aside.
8 oz. ricotta cheese	Beat until smooth and set aside.
½ cup Parmesan cheese	Set aside.
Approx. 4 cups prepared tomato sauce	

Assembly

Spread ¾ cup sauce in bottom of pan. Cover with 3 lasagna sheets. Spread half the ricotta over lasagna. Sprinkle half the mozzarella and Parmesan cheese over ricotta. Repeat layering with 1 cup sauce, lasagna noodles, and 3 cheeses. Spread remaining sauce over last of the lasagna noodles and bake, uncovered, approx. 1 hour. Let stand 10 minutes before cutting.

Per serving (⅛th)	
Calories:	274
Protein:	17 g
Fat:	9 g
Cholesterol:	30 mg
Carbohydrates:	30 g
Sodium:	423 mg

Clam Lasagna

This is a delicious and unusual lasagna filled with baby clams, spinach, and cheese.

Preheat oven to 350°F
Spray a 9″ × 13″ baking pan
with nonstick vegetable coating
Serves 8

Approx. 9–10 lasagna sheets	Cook in boiling water. Drain, rinse, and set aside. Meanwhile, prepare filling.
Approx. 16 oz. chopped spinach	Cook just until done, strain well. Set aside.
2 cups ricotta cheese	Set aside.
8 oz. thinly sliced mozzarella cheese	Set aside.
¼ cup Parmesan cheese	Set aside.
2 small cans of clams (5½–6½ oz. can)	Drain clams and save liquid. Set aside.
1 tbsp. margarine	Melt in saucepan.
4 tbsp. flour	Add, mix, and cook for 1 minute.
⅔ cup bottled clam juice (or fish stock)	Add along with reserved clam liquid. Cook until mixture boils and thickens, approx. 4 minutes. Remove from heat.

(continued)

Per serving (⅛th)	
Calories:	365
Protein:	27 g
Fat:	13 g
Cholesterol:	60 mg
Carbohydrates:	34 g
Sodium:	357 mg

Clam Lasagna *(continued)*

3 crushed garlic cloves
¹/₂ tsp. each dried basil,
oregano, thyme
¹/₄ cup chopped parsley
2 tbsp. lemon juice
dash of pepper

Stir into above along with reserved clams.

Assembly

Place 3 sheets lasagna in pan. Place half ricotta cheese, half the spinach, half the mozzarella and a third of the clam sauce. Repeat layers and top with remaining lasagna noodles, clam sauce, and Parmesan. Bake, uncovered, for 30 minutes or until bubbly and heated through. Let stand 10 minutes before serving.

Fusilli with Stir-Fried Beef and Vegetables

A delightful Oriental stir-fry pasta.

Serves 5

½ lb. fusilli (twisted pasta)	Cook in boiling water until al dente (firm to the bite). Drain and set aside.

Sauce

½ tbsp. grated ginger root *1 clove crushed garlic* *⅓ cup plus 2 tbsp. soy sauce* *1 cup plus 2 tbsp. boiling water*	Combine in small bowl.

Stir fry

1 tsp. oil *(preferably sesame oil)*	Heat in large pan or wok over high heat.
8 oz. good quality steak, *cut in thin strips*	Add beef and quickly brown. Add above sauce.
1 cup onion, cut into strips *1 cup carrots, cut into small pieces* *1 cup broccoli florets* *1 cup mushrooms, sliced (preferably oyster)* *1 cup snow peas*	Add and simmer 5 minutes, stirring occasionally.
2 cups bean sprouts *¼ tsp. black pepper* *dried crushed chili pepper to taste*	Add to above along with pasta and simmer 3 minutes. Serve.

Per serving (⅕th)

Calories:	360
Protein:	24 g
Fat:	9 g
Cholesterol:	42 mg
Carbohydrates:	48 g
Sodium:	1528 mg

198

Fettuccine Alfredo

A wide array of crisp vegetables in a creamy, light broth.

Serves 4

	1¹/₂ cups chicken stock	Boil until reduced to half, approx. 3 minutes. Set aside to cool.
	2 shallots or green onions, chopped (white part only) **¹/₄ cup chopped parsley** **¹/₂ cup white wine**	In a medium saucepan add ingredients and bring to a boil until reduced to half, approx. 2 minutes. Strain and save liquid in small bowl.
	¹/₄ cup evaporated skim milk **1 tbsp. flour** **salt and pepper**	Mix together and add cooled chicken stock. Add to wine mixture and bring to a boil over a low heat. Cook for approx. 3–5 minutes.
	2 tbsp. Parmesan cheese	Remove from heat and add cheese. Set sauce aside.
	1 medium carrot, sliced thin **1¹/₂ cups chopped broccoli** **1¹/₂ cups chopped cauliflower** **1 cup sliced mushrooms** **¹/₂ medium red pepper, thinly sliced** **¹/₄ cup fresh or frozen green peas**	In boiling water cook just until nearly done, approx. 3 minutes. Drain and set aside.
	¹/₂ lb. fettuccine (preferably whole wheat)	Cook in boiling water until al dente (firm to the bite). Drain and combine with vegetables and sauce. Toss well.

Per serving (¹/₄th)

Calories:	300
Protein:	13 g
Fat:	3 g
Cholesterol:	6 mg
Carbohydrates:	56 g
Sodium:	451 mg

Fettuccine with Sweet Peppers and Sun-Dried Tomatoes

A mild sauce enriched with olives, red peppers, and sun-dried tomatoes.

Serves 4

¹/₂ lb. fettuccine	Cook in boiling water until al dente (firm to the bite). Drain and set aside. Meanwhile, prepare sauce.
1 medium roasted red pepper, * sliced **15 sun-dried tomatoes, cut in half** **1 tsp. garlic** **2 green onions, chopped** **¹/₄ cup sliced black olives** **pinch of black pepper**	Place all ingredients in large, hot skillet and cook for 1 minute.
1¹/₂ cups chicken stock	Add slowly to above, stirring often on a moderate heat for approx. 3 minutes.
³/₄ cup prepared tomato sauce	Add and cook until thickened, approx. 5 minutes. Add pasta, toss, and serve.

*Under the broiler, roast pepper until charred. Cool under water, peel, and slice.

Per serving (¹/₄th)	
Calories:	260
Protein:	9 g
Fat:	1 g
Cholesterol:	0 mg
Carbohydrates:	54 g
Sodium:	429 mg

Pasta with Cheese Sauce and Vegetables

Soft, mild cheese melted over
vegetables and pasta.

Serves 4

½ lb. fettuccine (preferably spinach pasta)	Cook in boiling water until al dente (firm to the bite). Drain and set aside. Meanwhile, prepare sauce.
2 tsp. olive oil	Heat in large skillet.
¾ cup sliced mushrooms **¾ cup diced onion** **½ cup diced green pepper** **¾ tbsp. dry basil** **1 tsp. dry oregano**	Add and sauté just until vegetables are soft. Remove from heat. Set aside.
1¼ cups 2% or skim milk	Heat in saucepan.
1 tbsp. cornstarch or arrowroot **1–2 tbsp. cold water**	In a small cup, combine cornstarch and water until smooth. Add to milk and stir until thickened.
½ cup grated mild soft cheese (i.e., Monterey Jack, Havarti, brick, etc.) **pepper to taste** **2 tbsp. Parmesan** **paprika to taste**	Add to above and stir until smooth. Add pasta and vegetables, then toss and serve.

Per serving (¼th)

Calories:	363
Protein:	15 g
Fat:	10 g
Cholesterol:	22 mg
Carbohydrates:	53 g
Sodium:	167 mg

Linguine with Cheese and Tomatoes

*A light pasta tossed with a
variety of cheeses and herbs.*

Preheat oven to 400°F
Serves 5

8 oz. linguine

Cook in boiling water until al dente (firm to the bite). Drain and set aside.

1½ cups plum tomatoes, diced
⅓ cup finely chopped onion
½ cup goat cheese, crumbled
¼ cup Asiago * cheese, crumbled

Combine in casserole dish.

1 cup grated low-fat mild cheese
(i.e., mozzarella, Havarti, etc.)

Add ⅔ cup low-fat cheese and mix with above, saving other third for topping.

1 tbsp. mixed fresh herbs, chopped (rosemary, sage, thyme, oregano, or 1 tsp. mixed dry)
salt and pepper to taste
1 egg white

Add to the casserole dish above and mix. Add pasta, combine, and top with remaining low-fat cheese. Bake approx. 15 minutes, just until hot.

*If Asiago cheese is unavailable, substitute a hard, sharp white cheese, such as Romano or Parmesan.

Per serving (⅕th)
Calories: 361
Protein: 22 g
Fat: 12 g
Cholesterol: 7 mg
Carbohydrates: 40 g
Sodium: 384 mg

202

Pasta with Ricotta Cheese and Vegetables

*A wonderful pasta dish
for a light lunch or appetizer.*

Serves 4

½ lb. rotini (spiral pasta) (preferably whole wheat)	Cook in boiling water until al dente (firm to the bite). Meanwhile, prepare sauce.
1 tbsp. olive oil	Heat in large pan.
1 garlic clove, crushed *½ cup green peppers, sliced*	Sauté until tender.
2 cups sliced mushrooms	Add and sauté until done.
¾ cup corn kernels *1 cup broccoli, cut into small pieces*	Add to above, cover, and cook until broccoli is just cooked, approx. 5 minutes.
1 cup cherry tomatoes, halved *1 cup ricotta cheese* *4 green onions, chopped* *salt and pepper*	Add to above and cook until entire mixture is hot. Add rotini, toss, and serve.

Per serving (¼th)	
Calories:	379
Protein:	17 g
Fat:	9 g
Cholesterol:	19 g
Carbohydrates:	58 g
Sodium:	89 mg

Fettuccine with Seafood

Mixed seafood in a white wine sauce.

Serves 4

½ lb. fettuccine	Cook in boiling water until al dente (firm to the bite). Drain and set aside. Meanwhile, prepare sauce.
½ large onion, thinly sliced *1 leek (white part), thinly sliced* *⅓ cup chicken stock*	Cook, covered, in large saucepan until onion and leeks are tender.
¼ cup white wine *salt and red pepper to taste* *½ cup low-fat milk, hot*	Add and simmer, uncovered, for approx. 15–20 minutes, stirring frequently. Remove from heat.
½ tsp. lemon juice *8 oz. any combination of cooked seafood (shrimp, crab, scallops, or lobster)* *⅓ cup Parmesan cheese*	Add to above and mix well. Add pasta, toss, and serve.

Per serving (¼th)	
Calories:	329
Protein:	23 g
Fat:	4 g
Cholesterol:	64 mg
Carbohydrates:	50 g
Sodium:	309 mg

Angel Hair Pasta with Shrimp in a Tomato Pesto Sauce

A great combination of ingredients over fine strands of pasta.

Serves 6

¹⁄₂ cup white wine *1 lb. shrimp, shelled and deveined*	Poach until just barely cooked. Remove from pan, save liquid, and set aside.
10 oz. angel hair pasta (capellini)	Cook in boiling water until firm to the bite (al dente). Drain and set aside.

Sauce

1 tbsp. olive oil *2 small onions, chopped* *1 green pepper, chopped* *¹⁄₂ cup white wine* *1 lb. mushrooms, chopped* *12 small tomatoes, puréed*	Sauté onions and pepper in large saucepan for 5 minutes. Add wine and mushrooms to above along with reserved liquid from shrimp and cook for 2 minutes. Add puréed tomatoes.
4 tsp. dry oregano *3 tsp. dry basil* *1 bay leaf* *1 tsp. honey*	Add to above and simmer approx. 20–30 minutes, until thick.
1 tbsp. tomato paste	Add and cook another 10 minutes. Set aside.

Pesto Sauce

¹⁄₄ cup walnuts *2¹⁄₂ cups fresh basil* *3 cloves garlic* *2 tbsp. Parmesan* *1 tbsp. olive oil*	Purée until well-blended into a smooth paste. Add 4 tbsp. of this pesto to sauce. Refrigerate or freeze remainder for later use.

Assembly

Add shrimp and pasta to sauce, toss, and serve.

Per serving (¹⁄₆th)

Calories:	344
Protein:	22 g
Fat:	7 g
Cholesterol:	85 mg
Carbohydrates:	51 g
Sodium:	106 mg

Linguine with Salmon, Leeks, and Dill

*Fresh salmon pieces with leeks
in a light cream sauce.*

Serves 6

**10 oz. linguine (preferably
green spinach pasta)**

Cook in boiling water until firm
to the bite (al dente). Drain and
set aside. Meanwhile, prepare
sauce.

White Sauce

**dash cayenne pepper
$\frac{1}{4}$ tsp. nutmeg
2 cups low-fat milk**

Combine in saucepan and heat
just until boiling. Remove from
heat.

**$1\frac{1}{2}$ tbsp. flour
(preferably whole wheat)
1 tbsp. olive oil**

In another saucepan, over
medium heat, combine and mix
until a thick paste is reached.
Add above milk mixture and stir
constantly, until a thick sauce is
formed, approx. 5 minutes.

$\frac{1}{4}$ cup Parmesan cheese

Add, combine, and set aside.

**$\frac{1}{4}$ cup wine
2 tbsp. chopped shallots or onions
2 cloves crushed garlic
2 leeks, sliced in thin rounds**

Heat in another saucepan until
leeks become soft, approx. 10
minutes.

12 oz. salmon fillet, cubed

Add to above wine mixture
along with above milk sauce and
cook just until salmon is slightly
undercooked, approx. 2–3
minutes.

**3 tbsp. fresh dill, chopped
(1 tsp. dry)
sprinkle of crushed peppercorns (preferably pink)**

Add to above and combine.
Spoon over pasta, toss, and
serve.

Per serving (⅙th)	
Calories:	344
Protein:	22 g
Fat:	7 g
Cholesterol:	24 mg
Carbohydrates:	46 g
Sodium:	155 mg

Pasta with Spinach and Seafood Sauce

Seafood sauce over pasta stuffed with goat cheese and spinach.

Serves 4

4 manicotti shells or 4 sheets of lasagna 5″ × 4″	Cook in boiling water until al dente (firm to the bite). Drain, rinse with cold water, and set aside.
1 lb. shrimp (peel shrimp, reserve shells and set shrimp aside) 2 tbsp. rice 1 medium carrot, chopped 1 small onion, chopped 1 shallot (or green onion), chopped 1 stalk celery, chopped ¼ tsp. thyme 1 sprig parsley	In medium saucepan, add shells to the following ingredients, bring to a boil, then simmer, covered, for 25 minutes. Purée and pour back into saucepan.
1¼ cups chicken stock	Add to puréed mixture, stir. Press through a coarse sieve, pressing hard to obtain sauce.
dash of hot pepper (cayenne) 1 tsp. lemon juice 1 tsp. cognac (optional)	Add to above and set aside. In the meantime, cook the reserved shrimp in the method of your choice and set aside.
1 lb. fresh spinach	Cook half the spinach in boiling water just until wilted. Drain, chop, and squeeze out moisture.

(continued)

Per serving (¼th)

Calories:	305
Protein:	30 g
Fat:	4 g
Cholesterol:	106 mg
Carbohydrates:	37 g
Sodium:	529 mg

Pasta with Spinach and Seafood Sauce *(continued)*

¹/₂ cup goat cheese (chevre)   Add to above spinach and mix well. Set aside. Cook remaining spinach in boiling water until wilted. Drain, chop, and squeeze out moisture. Divide this spinach among four plates. Carefully place goat cheese and spinach mixture into pasta shells and place over spinach on plates. Reheat sauce if necessary and pour over pasta. Serve immediately, with cooked shrimp.

ALLEGRO—BOSTON

In 1981 Jim and Bonnie Burke took a working-class bar and turned it into a dining room which served fine Italian food. In those days their idea was revolutionary. Now more than ten years later Allegro, a Boston area restaurant, still has diners lining up for its innovative cuisine. Chef Jim Burke has a knack for raising the ordinary to the extraordinary and pleasing even the most discerning palate. The location has moved down the road and has a bar and waiting room for the ever-growing crowds.

ANDREA'S RESTAURANT—NEW ORLEANS

When dining on northern Italian food at Andrea's Restaurant in Louisiana, one is never certain if the dish ordered is Queen Elizabeth's favorite or the one that former-President Carter had. Chef Andrea Apuzzo has created meals for these famous people and many more. Born on the Isle of Capri, Apuzzo traveled the world before settling in Louisiana to open his restaurant. Apuzzo is a member of the International Wine and Food Society and has worked in famous kitchens around the world.

ANTHONY'S, TONY'S—HOUSTON

What do you get when you combine American southwestern influences with traditional Italian cuisine? Anthony's, a Houston restaurant, serving hot (as in "sought after") Italian food. Anthony's is the second of three restaurants (one of his other restaurants—Tony's—is also represented in this book) owned by Texas restaurateur Tony Vallone, who, together with Chef Bruce McMillian, has created a popular place—voted one of the top national restaurants—that does not lower its standards. Pastas are tender and desserts sumptuous—if you can get a seat. The Rigatoni with Roasted Tomato Sauce is especially delicious.

AVANZARE—CHICAGO

In the heart of Chicago's creative center is a northern Italian restaurant that is itself a work of art. Avanzare, with its granite walls, bronze Virginio

Ferrari sculptures, and bilevel dining room, serves wonderfully creative food. Northern Italian fare never tasted better than it does in the hands of Chef John Chiakulas. Under his direction the food has been simplified—pared down to its essence—allowing it to speak for itself. Experimental specials enhance the regular classic menu, adding an air of the unknown to this continually dependable restaurant.

BIFFI BISTRO—TORONTO
Ten years after opening, Biffi Bistro holds its place as one of the most popular spots in Toronto. People still line up to get in. Those who are initiated into this club—with its open-style kitchen playing to the celebrity crowds—are appreciative of the relaxed but elegant surroundings. Named after a Milan bistro, Biffi introduced Toronto to sophisticated northern Italian cuisine. Owner Corrado Furlanetto and Chef Michael Gillespie stay on top of culinary trends by traveling to major American food centers, keeping Biffi a top restaurant.

THE BLUE FOX—SAN FRANCISCO
When Gianni Fassio bought The Blue Fox, it was like coming home. This San Francisco restaurant has been in his family since the late forties, and Fasio spent most of his youth simmering soup and other delectables in this famed spot. Fassio gave up a prestigious accounting career to renovate The Fox and return it to its days of splendor. The food is pure artistry and does to the palate what it does to the eye—dazzles it. The wine list is weighted toward more obscure Italian wines, and the atmosphere is luxurious, with room between tables and classic European service.

THE BRASS ELEPHANT—BALTIMORE
The surroundings at The Brass Elephant in Baltimore are so beautiful you may never want to leave the dining room. Inhabiting a restored Victorian house—complete with hand-carved doors, a Moroccan teakwood balcony, and ceilings and mouldings carved by famous artists—The Brass Elephant offers both a visual and an edible feast. Elephant sconces and brass light fixtures name this restaurant, which was voted one of the top ten dining spots in *Baltimore Magazine*'s annual restaurant poll. The rich Italian food

is elegantly presented, and diners can always enjoy an exquisite detail upon which to cast the eye.

CAFÉ DE MEDICI—VANCOUVER

Gino Punzo, owner of Café de Medici, immigrated to Canada from Italy in 1955, bringing with him all the old-world charm and sophistication needed to create a restaurant worthy of the Medici name. Located in the center of Vancouver, Punzo's restaurant caters to the classic northern Italian palate, serving elaborate food in a formal setting. But at Café de Medici, traditional ways strike a perfect balance between formal and casual, keeping this restaurant elegant yet warm and inviting.

CAFÉ DES ARTISTES—NEW YORK

In the early 1900s Café des Artistes served as a home away from home for artists who lived and worked in the Upper West Side of Manhattan. Its mural of frolicking nymphs, painted by one of the more prominent artists of the time, Howard Chandler Christy, has been carefully restored, making this one of the most romantic spots in New York. This three-star restaurant, owned and operated by restaurant consultant George Lang, serves sumptuous food to the delight of its followers. And although a popular spot with celebrities, Café des Artistes is as warm and welcoming to the unknown patron as it is to a head of state.

CAFÉ TREVI—NEW YORK

At Café Trevi, an Upper East Side Manhattan restaurant, neighborhood patrons who saunter in to relax after a hard day's work think of it as "their" place. Down-to-earth food and a relaxed atmosphere encourage this kind of familiarity. But beware, for this popular spot is small—only fifty-five seats—and fills quickly. Although the food is conventional Italian, it is so well prepared that the experience is serendipitous and one you'll want to rediscover over and over again.

CAL-A-VIE—CALIFORNIA

Tucked away in a serene setting replete with colorful flowers on acres of rolling hills in North San Diego, Cal-a-Vie Health and Fitness Spa was designed and developed by founder William F. Power as a sanctuary for combating the high tide of stress and ill health in America. Catering to a maximum of twenty-four, this spa develops programs to suit the needs of each client, including fitness, nutrition, massage, and a variety of European body and skin therapies. The low-calorie cuisine boasts fresh herbs and vegetables from Cal-a-Vie's own garden, with healthy entrees like Linguine with Salmon, Leeks and Dill, and Angel Hair Pasta with Shrimp in a Tomato Pesto Base.

CANYON RANCH—ARIZONA & MASSACHUSETTS
If you're overweight, stressed out to the point of ulcers, and think life isn't worth living unless it tastes good, then Canyon Ranch is the place for you. One time mega-developer Mel Zuckerman was in just such a state when he found a spa to help him tone his life down. Then he founded his own spa, Canyon Ranch. The menu, with its emphasis on light cuisine, was developed by Jeanne Jones, who is an author, syndicated newspaper columnist, and light cuisine expert. Her food is light and delicious and would do a sensualist proud. Canyon Ranch has two locations situated in the mountains, with views that approximate Shangri-La.

CARLO'S RESTAURANT—SAN RAFAEL
Carlo's Restaurant is a reprieve from the sleek, trendy restaurants populating the culinary scene these days, and it offers first-rate Italian food in an informal, out-of-the-way cottage in San Rafael. Owned and operated by Carlo and Marie Avola, the restaurant's emphasis is on quality; it uses the freshest of local ingredients selected and prepared by Carlo. Marie takes over the dining room, transforming the eclectic surroundings into a warm, intimate, bustling space. Carlo's specialty is pasta and two of his best dishes are Spicy Fettuccine with Sweet Peppers and Penne with Dried Mushrooms.

CENTRO—TORONTO
Simple and elegant California-style Italian fare is the recipe for success at Centro, the latest creation of Toronto's preeminent restaurateur, Franco Prevedello. This midtown haunt attracts an eclectic group of patrons; local glitterati line the curbs with limousines while neighborhood gourmands

stroll to Centro three and four times a week. Ephemeral decor, a superbly stocked wine bar, and the latest in haute cuisine make Centro a unique combination of successful ingredients. And, as with any recipe, the best ingredients yield the best results.

CHIANTI RISTORANTE—LOS ANGELES

Sepia murals of Tuscany and the original wooden booths are reminders of the glorious past in Chianti, a restaurant that some claim is the oldest Italian eatery in Los Angeles. First opening its doors in 1938, Chianti became a haven for celebrities who found they could dine there without being mauled by the press. This bastion of old-world dining, spruced up since its inception, still serves up some of the best classic Italian food in town. And if you're worried about being seen, don't. Well-known stars are still protected from the papparazzi.

CITY RESTAURANT—LOS ANGELES

City Restaurant, located on a once-forgotten stretch of LaBrea Avenue in Los Angeles, has been a focal point of the area's revitalization. Now surrounded by galleries and fashionable shops, City remains at the forefront of American Cuisine. Chef Susan Feninger's preparation technique is classic French, and her unique, eccentric menu features peasant food inspired by travels to Thailand, India, and Japan. The resulting City Cuisine is an astoundingly simple, straightforward approach to global dining.

DA MARCELLO—MONTREAL

Like a painter who would never paint the same thing twice, Marcello Banini, chef and owner of Da Marcello in Montreal, creates a new menu every night. Banini, who has been cooking since he was a child, says he cooks Tuscan food in his restaurant because "it's the most romantic." For his culinary inspiration, Banini travels back to Italy every year searching, like a scholar, for recipes to bring home. The seating is limited—only sixteen tables—and one can frequent the restaurant for years without ever having the same meal twice.

DALESIO'S—BALTIMORE

Located in a townhouse in Baltimore's little Italy, Dalesio's serves up some of the best Italian food in town. Its proximity to Chesapeake Bay ensures fresh

213

seafood, and local markets supply the produce. Dalesio's also offers a spa menu—with no salt, refined sugars, or fat or cholesterol. Fresh, natural juices are served from the bar, and only natural spring water is available. Some of the recipes (Linguine with Chicken and Mushrooms and Sun-Dried Tomatoes) call for whole wheat pasta, but for those less health conscious, regular pasta will do.

DANIEL'S—TUCSON

Being the youngest son of Tucson's restaurant dynasty and opening his own place in the same town could have been a fatal mistake for Daniel Scordato, owner of Daniel's. Lucky for us, it wasn't. One of the best Italian restaurants in this area, Daniel's is tamed by its sophistication. This blend of old and new creates some intriguing cuisine. The decor is elegant—black and ivory with highlights of teal and coral—and separate dining rooms are perfect for formal or intimate dining. Whole Red Peppers Stuffed with Capellini and Prosciutto Ham is testament to Daniel's preeminence.

THE DONATELLO—SAN FRANCISCO

It's not every day that a hotel is named after a restaurant, but that is exactly what happened when Pacific Plaza was renamed The Donatello, in honor of the award-winning restaurant. Classically inspired Italian cuisine abounds in this kitchen, with Chef Luigi Mavica paying tribute to Italy's regional foods. The extensive wine list is exceptional, and the two dining rooms are warm and intimate; hand-painted fabric covers the walls of one, and the other is replete with Carrara marble.

DORAL SATURNIA—FLORIDA

Blending American fitness techniques with soothing European treatments, Doral Saturnia, a lavish Florida spa, is committed to healing both body and soul. The emphasis is on balance, and Doral Saturnia works toward that harmony. The Spa Centre and luxury Spa Villa are reminiscent of Tuscany, with remarkable reproductions of Botticelli masterpieces transporting you back to Italy. Fitness programs incorporate exercise on land and water, with stress reduction utilizing a whole range of water and body therapies. The pasta, like Fettuccine Alfredo, has all the taste of a fine Italian dish, but is reduced in both calories and fat.

GALILEO—WASHINGTON

As you walk into Galileo's, a Washington, D.C., restaurant, you'll notice the sun streaming through the arches, dividing the large, lively dining room into intimate corners. Authentic northern Italian cuisine of the highest quality is served from this kitchen, and it begins with the grilled bruschetta proffered at your table. Chef-owner Roberto Donna cooks it all—fish, meat, pasta, and desserts from heaven—resulting in some of the most inventive cuisine in the city. Ingratiate your friends with the Tortellini with Creamy Cheese Sauce—a truly heavenly experience.

GIULIANO'S—CARMEL

At Giuliano's, traditional northern Italian cuisine is truly a family affair. Susan and Robert Negri, together with sons Michael (maitre d') and Scott (chef), operate the restaurant. In 1981 they took this former Laundromat and turned it into an intimate, elegant restaurant, serving superb food with that extra something that comes from a family kitchen. Eschewing "new California" cooking, Scott prefers resurrecting family recipes passed on during summer visits to the northern Italian town of Chiaverano. Scott Negri likes things simple: "A restaurant's food should stand on its own." And at Giuliano's, it always does.

THE HEARTLAND—ILLINOIS

At The Heartland Health and Fitness Retreat/Spa, situated among the farmlands of Illinois, twenty-seven guests gather each week to partake in the most advanced methods known to reshape both body and mind. The high-powered clientele are encouraged to not only reduce their fat intake and increase their aerobic activity, but to practice stress management by learning the difference between good and bad stress. Massage and other pampering services are available to encourage relaxation, and the food— low-fat, low-cal vegetarian—is sure to do its part to help you reduce. Try the Vegetable Lasagna or Linguine Toscano for a light and delicious meal.

IL CANTINORI—NEW YORK

As you walk into Il Cantinori, a Manhattan Village restaurant, you are greeted by a colorful display of cold antipasti that may well end up at your table as a first course. A spacious restaurant, Il Cantinori nonetheless boasts an intimate feel: it features a rustic atmosphere and a bar that divides the large restaurant into two dining rooms. Often a spot for the artsy crowd, Il Cantinori is busy all the time, and reservations are necessary. The menu is large and offers abundant choice, but daily specials guide diners to the freshest dishes.

IL FORNAIO—SAN FRANCISCO

It is said that you can tell the quality of a restaurant by the bread it serves. Il Fornaio, originally a bakery chain in Italy intent on teaching the vanishing art of bread making, is a great restaurant. With over a thousand bakeries in Europe, Il Fornaio found its way into the United States in 1980 and opened its first full-service restaurant in 1987. Since then a group of Il Fornaio restaurants, all dedicated to the principle of preserving authentic Italian cuisine, have opened. And at each one, the bread and the food are divine.

IL MULINO—NEW YORK

The only problem with Il Mulino, a Greenwich Village Italian restaurant, is that it's too popular. Passionate fans wait patiently at the bar of this cramped eatery, even if they have reservations. Their patience is rewarded with wonderfully robust food redolent with garlic. The atmosphere is typical of Village restaurants, with low lighting making it difficult to read. Never mind, however: the only necessity in this superb restaurant is the ability to taste.

IL NIDO/IL MONELLO—NEW YORK

Addi Giovanetti, one of the first restaurateurs to serve northern Italian fare in Manhattan and owner of Il Nido and Il Monello, is intent on pleasing your palate. Customer satisfaction is what these restaurants are all about. If choosing from the menu is too difficult after a long day at the office, Giovanetti will orchestrate a sumptuous meal designed to fit your mood. After dinner, amble over to Il Nido Café and take some of this wonderful food home.

IL POSTO—TORONTO

Consistency and superb quality attract an elite clientele to Il Posto, a northern Italian restaurant in the heart of Toronto. Nella and Piero Maritanos prepare dishes minutes before they're served, and the homemade pasta is sauced seconds before it arrives at the table. An extensive wine list and intimate atmosphere make Il Posto one of the most exclusive restaurants in Toronto. While dining, the only sounds one hears are the contented sighs of diners and the dessert-laden trolly discreetly making its way from one table to the next.

KING RANCH—TORONTO
Designed by renowned Canadian architect Arthur Erickson, King Ranch is located on 177 acres of lush, wooded countryside within thirty minutes of Toronto. The guest experience is one of "having your batteries recharged" within a fresh and natural environment of healthy living. The clubhouse, 120-room guest residences, and spa were designed to harmonize with the landscape and offer endless opportunities for relaxation and rejuvenation. Spa programs are comprehensive, and the changing seasons offer an extensive range of activities to accommodate every guest. Executive Chef Chris Klugman has created cuisine that is light and satisfying and, with recipes like Fusilli with Stir-Fried Beef and Vegetables, never dull.

LA RIVIERA—NEW ORLEANS
Chef Goffredo Fraccaro's travels to many countries have netted him a world of experience, and he brings this experience to La Riviera, his Italian restaurant in New Orleans. His cooking is inventive and imaginative; he has created dishes like Crabmeat Ravioli and taken the top prize in San Francisco's Crabmeat Olympics. His list of awards is impressive, including the Italian government's Oscar for Outstanding Achievement, the first ever presented to a chef.

LA SILA—MONTREAL
The freshest of ingredients are demanded by Antoine Donato, owner and chef of La Sila. Named after a mountain range in his home region of Calabria, La Sila attracts an eclectic group of patrons who come together for a taste of the exquisite. Not a regionalist, Donato harvests recipes from all parts of Italy. Located in Sherbrooke, La Sila's decor is cozy. And, like the mountain range it recalls, it shelters you, if only for a short time, from the outside world.

217

LA TOUR (PARK-HYATT)—CHICAGO

Ensconced in the luxurious Hyatt Hotel, La Tour is exceptional in its own right. Handpainted murals on the wall and a view of Water Tower Square through two-story-high windows set the scene for this culinary feast. In the lobby is a caviar bar—beluga served on miniblinis and washed down with lemon- or pepper-spiked vodka—to whet your appetite. Once you enter the dining room, the delights continue. Executive Chef Charles Webber has invented an exciting menu creative enough to please the most demanding gourmets. And like everything else in this restaurant, the wine list is world class, with more than three thousand bottles of the best vintages from all major regions of the world.

LOCANDA VENETA—LOS ANGELES

In a city where Italian restaurants abound, Locanda Veneta is a beacon for those seeking something unique. Chef Antonio Tommasi, a native of the region of Veneta, cooks this distinct regional cuisine exclusively in his Los Angeles restaurant. The three-star dining room is tiny and often crowded, but rather than being an annoyance, this merely adds to the serendipitous pleasure of Tommasi's food. With an open kitchen tantalizing the senses, dining at Locanda Veneta can transport you to a different time and a different place.

MICHELA'S—BOSTON

Innovative food and a high-tech environment in an offbeat location could be disastrous in unskilled hands, but at Michela's the hands are quite skilled and the results superb. Owner Michela Larson works closely with her chef, creating exciting Italian fare for an upscale clientele. She is ever present in the dining room, ensuring that her customers are well taken care of. And though this popular Cambridge restaurant has received numerous awards for its hearty, country-style cuisine, patrons are always warmly welcomed and made to feel at home.

MOMO'S ITALIAN SPECIALTIES—DALLAS

It's difficult to find Italian restaurants that serve authentic cuisine in Dallas, so Momo's Italian Specialties—with three restaurant locations—is a particular delight. Owner and Chef Antonio Gattini has been called the most authentic Italian chef in Dallas. The restaurants attest to his skill as a chef and restaurateur, with Momo's boasting a large repeat business. And at his newest restaurant, Gattini has enlarged his repertoire to include risotto, polenta, and more of his heavenly pastas. Try Spaghetti with Escargots, an exotic yet affordable dish.

MONTE CARLO LIVING ROOM—PHILADELPHIA

Located in the Society Hill area of Philadelphia, Monte Carlo Living Room is a throwback to the time when a restaurant's elegance was the only criterion by which accolades were meted out. Fortunately, at Monte Carlo Living Room the northern Italian food is superb and holds its own against the sophisticated surroundings. Elegant waiters delivering attentive service—ingredients are presented table side—making dining at Monte Carlo Living Room a unique and welcome experience. Especially nice is the Linguine with Yellow Pepper Sauce served over black and white pasta.

MOVENPICK—TORONTO

Movenpick, originally a Swiss restaurant and now a restaurant empire with locations all over the world, came to Canada in 1982 under the able hands of Jorg Reichert. Mr. Reichert and his wife, Marianne, moved to Toronto to oversee the first North American Movenpick. Steeped in old values like total customer satisfaction, Movenpick has been extraordinarily successful. Chef Christian Aerni's fantastic desserts lure both tourists and local diners. And for those not fortunate enough to have a Movenpick in their city, don't despair. More prospects are on the horizon.

ON BROADWAY RISTORANTE—FORT WORTH

Hidden in a shopping strip in southwest Fort Worth, On Broadway is a bustling place. Continental Italian cuisine is served in this congenial restaurant; moderate prices and a diverse menu make it a frequent spot for neighborhood locals. Pastas are homemade, the wine list is extensive, and specialty coffees—flames and all—delight the crowds. Crowds are what you find, but waiting at On Broadway has its rewards.

PALIO—NEW YORK

As you walk into Palio, a Manhattan restaurant owned by famed restaurateur Chef Andreas Hellrigel, you'll be overwhelmed by the Sandro Chia mural Palio, which depicts the famed horse race that runs through the city of Siena. The mural envelops the lower lobby bar area, where patrons come for a drink and snack after a day's work. A private elevator escorts diners to the second-story restaurant, where they dine on Hellrigel's ethereal food and partake of his world-class wine list. The ubiquitous Palio motif is a constant reminder that, while the restaurant is at the forefront of nouvelle cuisine, its roots are firmly planted in tradition.

PAOLA'S—NEW YORK

A small, romantic spot in Upper East Side Manhattan, Paola's quietly stands out—a remarkable achievement in New York, where restaurants are a dime a dozen. Owned and operated by Paola Marracino, this tiny restaurant is frequented by those living in this elegant, upscale area. What they discover at Paola's is wonderful northern Italian food served in a warm, congenial atmosphere. Fusilli with Artichokes and Tomatoes or Capellini with Asparagus and Scallops are two recipes sure to please you and your guests.

PRIMI/VALENTINO—LOS ANGELES

Piero Selvaggio, Los Angeles restaurateur extraordinaire, owns two of the most celebrated Italian restaurants in this part of the country: Primi and Valentino. Valentino's ethereal food and Primi's tapas-style menu are testimony to the creative and bold approach Selvaggio promotes in his restaurants. The boss is forever challenging his chefs to perfect their artistry, and patrons of his two restaurants reap the benefits, some of the best of which are the pastas. Selvaggio is philosophical when extolling the virtues of pasta, calling it a "universal" dish. An apt description by a man who creates out-of-this-world cuisine.

RISTORANTE PRIMAVERA—NEW YORK

Ristorante Primavera, an uptown Manhattan Italian restaurant that opened in 1979, was one of the first restaurants to abandon the ubiquitous tomato sauce of the seventies. Owner Nicola Civetta is a stickler for detail. Waiters clad in black dinner jackets are attentive but not overbearing, which seems just right for this limousine crowd. And it seems that Civetta has developed something of a cult following for his Roasted Marinated Goat. This dish, complete with fanciful fruit carvings which Civetta creates himself keeps them coming back.

SCOOZI—CHICAGO

It seems that some of the best entertainment in Chicago is in a converted garage where Scoozi, an Italian restaurant, is wildly busy and never dull. Crowded to the point of overflowing, Scoozi serves up trendy but good cuisine and offers most items in servings large enough for two. This large trattoria—with more than three hundred seats—is not for quiet conversation or romantic dinners, but with this much activity, people watching is superb.

SPIAGGIA—CHICAGO

Overlooking Lake Michigan, Spiaggia, the preeminent northern Italian restaurant in Chicago, is as breathtaking inside as it is outside. A veined marble archway with two-story floor-to-ceiling windows enhances the majestic view. Homemade food, including pastas, is the mainstay of Spiaggia, a recipient of the prestigious Ambassador Award in 1989. Pizzas are baked in wood-burning ovens, and pasta dishes abound, with daily pasta specials augmenting the already large menu. With an extensive wine list and desserts from heaven, the food does justice to the spectacular surroundings.

TOSCANO'S RESTAURANT—BOSTON

Chef-owner Vinicio Paoli has two superb northern Italian restaurants, one located in the Italian area of Boston and the other in Providence, Rhode Island. This Florence-born chef, who trained in five-star hotels in Italy, consistently produces authentic Italian cuisine in an area where impostors of the "real thing" abound. Eschewing typically garish surroundings, Toscano's interiors are sedate and unimposing. The menu is short, but every item is superbly created, upholding the old adage that less is more. Try his unique Linguine with Chickpea Sauce.

UMBERTO AL PORTO—VANCOUVER

Authentic Italian cuisine made Umberto Menghi's first restaurant a success in Vancouver in the days when spaghetti and meatballs were considered ethnic fare. Six restaurants later, Menghi is still working his magic, and that magic is ever present at his pasta emporium, Umberto al Porto. Fresh, reliable, inexpensive food is served in this converted gastown warehouse, which boasts a congenial atmosphere. A recipient of the Wine Spectator Award, Umberto al Porto's wine cellar is exceptional.

UPSTAIRS AT THE PUDDING—BOSTON

Housed in a setting steeped in tradition, Upstairs at the Pudding has created its own tradition: serving out-of-the-ordinary Italian food. The restaurant, with its enigmatic name, is housed above the Hasty Pudding Club near Harvard Square. Chef-owner Deborah Hughes is an expert at creating dishes grounded in traditional Italian cooking and filled with exotic ingredients from around the world. And unlike the club it rests upon, Upstairs at the Pudding is not a secret society; it's open to everyone.